World War II Combat Veterans of the

TORPEDOED FOR LIFE

"A Careless Word, a Needless Sinking" by Otto Fischer. Credit: Ohio Historical Society

because of Washington's total
Denial & Injustice
shown to Merchant Marine veterans
since WW II.

A FEW ARE STILL LIVING AND THIS IS THEIR STORY.

World War II Combat Veterans of the U.S. Merchant

TORPEDOED FOR LIFE

Dear Baby Brother here is a
copy of my last book I'll
probably I'll write.
my two previous books, much to
my surprise are still in print.
I'm sorry I didnt think of you
when this book hit the street.
    your Elder Brother
      Herman Gerald Starnes
    Sunday March 30, 2014

About the Author

H. Gerald Starnes, a native of Southwest Virginia, is a retired GE Field Engineer, Project & Customer Service Manager. He received his Bachelor of Science degree from the US Merchant Marine Academy in 1947, which was one of the first bachelor's degrees awarded at Kings Point. He holds a U.S. Coast Guard Chief Engineer's License, which he received in 1953, and he sailed seven years on T-2 tankers. He received his Master of Business Administration from Long Island University in NY in 1970.

He is a member of the American Merchant Marine Veterans (AMMV) and the National Association for Uniformed Services (NAUS). The AMMV honored him with a Distinguished Service Award in recognition of his long and outstanding service to the organization. He was also recognized for his diligent and tireless efforts to attain passage of HR-23, the "Belated Thank You for the Merchant Mariners of World War II Act of 2007."

He is the author of *Of Them That Left a Name Behind,* an 800-page history of the Starnes family - 1980, and Forrest's Forgotten Horse Brigadier, a 110-page paperback on Col. James W. Starnes, a Confederate Cavalry Commander, killed in action on June 30, 1863. It is a 1990 history reference. Gerry is very surprised that the two books are still in print. Heritage Books, Inc. 100 Railroad Ave. #104, Westminster, MD, (800) 876-6103.

About the Photographer

Ed Trester was born in Brooklyn N. Y. He left High School in 1944 after turning age 17 and enlisted in the U. S. Merchant Marine. He was sent to the U. S. Maritime school at Sheepshead Bay in Brooklyn N.Y. where trainees were taught the skills of seamanship in rapid order and found themselves on a ship at sea 3 weeks later. He was awarded the Atlantic, Mediterranean, and the Pacific War Zone Medals. After the war he went to work for Metropolitan life Insurance Co. in Jacksonville Florida as sales manager. A stern advocate for Merchant Marine veterans rights, he often holds meetings at local libraries on the role of the Merchant Marine in WW 11. He is also an accomplished musician playing drums in his swing band. He currently lives in St. Augustine Florida with his wife Maggi.

Ed Trester on family's front steps while on weekend leave from Maritime school.

Acknowledgments

A good number of Merchant Marine WW II combat veterans have stated their memories here about what they did on their ships for their country to supply the needs of our fighting men and those of our allies all over the earth. We are all now in our upper 80's & 90's and dealing with medical problems. No one knows how many of us are still alive. Every day we hear that one or more of our WW II sailor comrades have "Crossed the Bar" (passed away). There have probably been more than 50 Merchant Marine wartime books written over the years since the war. This one will probably be the last and we will tell our story up to the present. No one on the streets now has heard of these Merchant Mariners.

The War Shipping Administration accepted 15, 16 and 17 boys who lied about their age, disabled people aged 70 and anyone who could function on the vessels. They would be trained for a few short weeks at shore side training camps and then sent out to sea. Our shipyards in 1942 and 43 had to build Liberty and Victory ships, tankers and other vessels faster than the Germans and Japanese could sink them. The U.S. Merchant Marine Academy was approved and under construction at Kings Point, NY. Boys 17 and 18 who had finished high school and the state schools were selected to train there as cadets to quickly become ships' officers.

We are very proud to have stories about Stanley Willner in *Death's Railway* and Perry Adam in *Little Ships* which were written by Gerald Reminick and published by the Glencannon Press, Mr. Walter Jafffe, Publisher, El Cerritto, CA. These gentlemen have wished us well with this book. *The Forgotten Heroes,* by the well-known author, Mr. Brian Herbert, is the third book we used for expertise on total information about the Merchant Marine. We met Mr. Herbert at the April 18, 2007 House Committee on VA Affairs. He spoke strongly about the treatment and neglect the country had given us. When his verbal time ran out, he continued with a five-page written testimony.

This volume's publishing would not be possible without the collection of WW II Merchant Marine information provided by Captain Dave Swan of the St. Johns River Chapter of the AMMV from the Maritime Museum in Jacksonville, FL 32260. The subject of this book is not the U.S. in WW II. Those accounts almost never mention the Merchant Mariners. Our stories are told by these old men who were out there on every ocean before, during and after the US entered the war, 1940-1946. We most certainly acknowledge the contribution of their stories.

I could not have produced this work without the transcription and editing services of my dear wife, Etta Faye, who patiently and diligently kept the work going. Her special training in education served me well. Thank you, Etta Faye.

We want to thank the *Ohio Historical Society* for the use of their painting "A Careless Word, a Needless Sinking" by Otto Fischer, and *Project Liberty Ship* for their pictures, and a special thanks to Jerry Saia for his technical support.

Our objective is to provide a truthful story of the
U.S. Merchant Mariners' part in winning WW II from
the Axis warmongers and The National Disgrace of
their treatment from their country to this day.

Table of Contents

250,000 U.S. WW II Combat Veteran Heroes

Torpedoed for Life

Washington's Years of Denial and Injustice
shown to the Merchant Mariners
A Few Are Still Living and This Is Their Story

We began with George Washington's Revolutionary War Merchant Mariners as Privateers, the 1775 beginning of the US Merchant Marine a year before the U.S. Marine Corps. Most of the colonies had formed their own navies. For a while the General had his own force known as "George Washington's Navy." At that time the British Royal Navy was the largest and most feared force on earth. An act of Congress formed the Continental Navy of 31 ships to protect and defend the united colonies.

Through commissions, paperwork and Congress, merchant ship captains were given authority to intercept, destroy or commandeer British ships and cargo. The crews of these privateer vessels came from every country on the planet and included some black slaves. Much of the booty from the privateers supplied Washington's "rag tag" army with necessary materials of war. But the officers and crew members of those vessels were well paid and seen as fulfilling their military obligations.

American seamen captives who were held on ships by the British had a dreadful mortality rate. More than 11,000 captives on ships died. Americans received the worst treatment of all countrymen. They were insurrectional mutineers of "His Royal Majesty, George III."

George Washington did not treat colonial seamen with deserved respect. When prisoner exchanges were considered, he refused to trade any British soldiers or sailors for any of the sickly, gaunt American seamen.

After the Revolutionary War thousands of British seamen deserted the poor conditions they worked under to sign on American ships for a better life. The British policy response was known as "impressment" where they stopped American ships, searched them for deserters and took them into custody. They were forced to work on British naval and merchant ships and some had to fight in the ongoing war with Napoleon Bonaparte of France.

The War of 1812 was partially over "impressment" and fought by merchant seamen since the U.S. had almost no Navy, only seven frigates. Britain effectively blocked American ports and mistakenly left their homeland unprotected. 500 American Privateers captured thirty thousand British prisoners and more than 1,300 ships and cargoes.

At the time of the Mexican-American War in 1846, the seaward fortress city of Veracruz was considered the strongest fortress in the western hemisphere. In 1847, General Winfield Scott, a hero of the War of 1812, chartered ocean going ships manned by merchant seamen to carry troops and military supplies to a position on the coast only 12 miles south of the fortress. After one week of siege by U.S. land and naval batteries, the Mexicans surrendered the fortress and city. General Scott wanted to get going to the Capitol. Captain Robert E. Lee found the way in.

Our American Civil War started in 1861 and the decorated hero of the two previous wars, General Winfield Scott, presented President Lincoln with a sweeping strategy to defeat the southern Confederacy. The only part of this plan that Lincoln adopted was to blockade key rebel seaports: Starve them out by cutting off their imports of supplies and destroy their economy by preventing exports. The Union Navy had less than 100 obsolete warships. There's more than 3,500 miles of Confederate coastline from North Carolina to Texas. This required the Union Navy to take control of 600 merchant vessels, manned by 70,000 Merchant Mariners.

Surprising ingenuity was shown by the Confederates who had no industrial facilities to build large ocean-going ships. The British had laws against building warships for "belligerents." The South ordered unarmed merchant vessels under phony names as purchasers, then sailed to friendly ports where they were armed and sent into battle against the North as "commerce raiders." Northern politicians complained about a second ship referred to as "Number 290"under construction in Liverpool. On July 29, 1862, Raphael Simmes, its daring Captain, ordered everyone except crew members onto the tug boats and went out for a trial run, but he kept going to the Azores where the ship was refitted with armaments and re-commissioned as the Alabama. Simmes and his crew in 23 months destroyed 58 unarmed merchant vessels and sank a federal warship. In the end, Confederate raiders and privateers destroyed 257 Union ships.

During the Spanish-American war in 1898, the Merchant Marine had not recovered from the devastation of the Civil War. Commodore George Dewey attacked and destroyed the Spanish fleet at Manila Bay in the Philippines. Converted merchant ships carried 11,000 U.S. troops across the Pacific in five convoys. In mid-August 1898, they took control of the city of Manila and ended Spanish authority in the Philippines.

World War I had gone on for almost three years when the U.S. entered it in early April 1917. Congress ordered a massive merchant fleet shipbuilding program. More than160 shipyards began building 3,300 vessels. The war ended the next year before most of these ships had been finished and gone to sea. A class of slow ships was called "Hog Islanders" after the place where they were built. A few were still active when the Pearl Harbor attack put the U.S. into WW II.

In a famous speech on December 29, 1940, President Roosevelt declared that the U.S. "must be the great arsenal of democracy." Under that doctrine he vowed to provide Great Britain with armaments, fuel and food so they could not be isolated and starved into submission by the Germans. The British were facing starvation by that time in WW II. To accomplish this ambitious goal known as "Lend Lease" a steady stream of merchant ships across the Atlantic Ocean put American Merchant Mariners in harm's way. This was especially the case with cargoes of aviation gasoline, cotton and other highly flammable materials. They ran at night blacked out in a 100 to 200 ships convoy and the threat of a submarine "wolf pack attack." "Lend Loss" was the name some used, being unhappy about their risk as untrained civilians on lightly or unarmed merchant vessels for the benefit of our allied nations rather than the U.S. A number of American Mariners were killed, injured and captured as POWs before the Pearl Harbor Japanese attack and Adolph Hitler's declaration of war on the U.S.

Choice of Liberty Ship Engine

The Liberty Ship engine

Picture of the huge 140 ton triple-expansion
engine that powered the Liberty Ship.

President Roosevelt approved of the Liberty ship because of its functional delivery of any type of cargo but referred to them as "ugly ducklings" or "sitting ducks." A ship was considered a success if it delivered its whole cargo of war materials and was sunk afterward. These ships were based on a British design for cargo ships with a reciprocating steam engine that was modified by the Americans. With that "up and down" engine, the vessel could make no more speed than 11 knots "flat out." The "Black Gang" (Engineer, Oiler and Fireman-Water Tender) had to lubricate the hot running engine by hand and check its bearings' temperature by touch. Facilities to build more modern diesel or electric powered ships engines were just not available. Torpedoes were always fired at the ship's engine room to stop the vessel for a kill. More of the engine room crew members were killed and injured than those on deck. We knew that when we went on our four-hour watch in the noisy hot engine room that our country was at war. We were proud to be the guys who kept the engine and boiler going and all the lights on down below.

As early as February 1941 before our entry in WW II, German admirals were aware of the threat of the American Lend Lease merchant ships crossing the Atlantic to England. Adolf Hitler was convinced by his admirals that all available air and sea power against the convoys had to be used if they ever were going to defeat the British. They built disguised raider ships that looked like merchant ships. These axis raiders had many ways to conceal their ships, guns and armament. U-boat crews called it "the happy time." Many more than a thousand merchant seamen died in the Atlantic. These civilian volunteers' casualty rate was much higher than those of the armed forces, and these German ships sank hundreds of thousands of tons of allied shipping in 1942 and 1943. Their submarine captains had been merchant ship captains before the war and were familiar navigators in the Atlantic and Gulf of Mexico.

We have to remind ourselves that many if not most of our American merchant ships at this time had any or few armaments aboard. The Navy

Armed Guard did their best in combat. But it seemed like it took forever to get cannons, machine and anti-aircraft guns installed and the Merchant Mariners trained to work with the Armed Guard gunners. It was said that Fleet Admiral Ernest J. King during this terrible 1942-1943 period had five or six destroyers in his command that could have been fitted with depth charges and used to scare and destroy the German submarines. In mid-1943, President Roosevelt had to coerce Admiral King to provide a convoy for American merchant ships to a mid-ocean meeting point where the Royal Navy would escort them the rest of the way to English ports. Roosevelt had served as an Assistant Secretary in the U.S. Navy's organization during WW I and was respected as one who knew how the Navy had to function in wartime. He was an invalid.

Congress had been reluctant to arm merchant ships because of the additional cost. A Navy Armed Guard and their officer were placed on 1,350 merchant vessels where every man was a target. No one was immune from the consequences of a hit. Burning oil from ruptured tanks could blaze for hours and hours. Cold ocean water congealed unburned oil into large, thick pads that made swimming impossible. A torpedo from a sub or a bomb from enemy aircraft often destroyed the lifeboats and could make a vessel a flaming pyre.

Launching Ceremony

There were always huge crowds celebrating the birth of a new ship.

The *S.S. William Pepper* ready for launching

January 1943

No Preparation for War

The United States of America was absolutely and completely unprepared for war and we elderly vividly recall it all. Four months into the war the S.S. Gulf America, built at Sparrows Point, MD, was sailing north from Port Arthur, TX on her maiden voyage to NY with a cargo of 90,000 barrels of fuel oil on the warm spring night of April 10, 1942. Her complement was 41 Merchant Marine crew and 7 Naval Armed Guards. All the shore lights were burning brightly and armed U.S. Naval Forces were practically nonexistent on the Atlantic Coast. At Jacksonville Beach quite a few residents were looking out at sea and enjoying the fine weather.

Five miles off the beach about 10:20 p.m. the German U-boat 123 had been stalking the tanker for hours waiting for darkness. Commanded by Reinhart Hardegen it fired two torpedoes at close range on the starboard side of the Gulf America that set off a huge fire from the oil cargo and the ship's fuel tanks. The engineers were killed and the engine stopped.

Hardegen couldn't see the damage done from the attack for the smoke and fire and ordered the submarine to surface and go in close on the port side. Capt. Oscar Anderson had ordered an "Abandon Ship" and the crewmen were trying to get to the life boats and rafts to get away from the flaming oil on the water on that side of the fire. Deck guns on the U-boat began firing on these 25 men who were jumping into the oil and fire on the water to avoid being hit. The radio operator was sending out a distress call when the Germans shot down his antenna with a machine gun and killed him. Seeing that the S.S. *Gulf America* was sinking, the sub submerged and silently got away. Residents on the beach rushed down to the beach and tried to rescue the dying sailors with any boat they could find.

Survivors were left to the mercy of God and the sea. They could hear each other's screams and yells to one another as they tried to make their way through the thick bunker C boiler fuel oil from the ship's ruptured tank. Seventeen of the crew and two Naval Armed Guards were lost. A blackout of coast lights was ordered by the Florida Governor.

Unlike all the Armed Forces who formed Afro-Americans into their own separate units with white officers, the Merchant Marine did not discriminate against any race or background, physical condition or age if they were capable of performing their duties aboard their ship. Some few sailors of color made it to the rank of Captain and Chief Engineer. A good many boys 15 and 16 years of age as well as the elderly lied about their ages and were accepted. These were not acceptable to the Armed forces. Their ages varied from 15 into the 70's. Lost hands and arms, feet and legs and poor eyesight were okay. Other crew members could stand watch as lookouts. Those ships being built in shipyards all over the Atlantic, Pacific and Gulf coasts had to be manned. This is war and there are floating mines out there.

Four such Mariners of color lost their lives on the *Gulf America*. Robert J. Banks, 25, Messman; Michel J. Monohan, 49, Machinist; Richard A. Van Pelt, 20, Wiper and James K. Walker 32, 2nd Cook were honored by having four Liberty ships named for them.

Captain Hugh Nathaniel Mulzac

(L-R) C. Lastic, Second Mate;
T. J. Young, Midshipman;
E. B. Hlubik, Midshipman;
C. Blackman, Radio Operator;
T. A. Smith, Chief Engineer

Hugh Mulac, Captain;
Adolphus Fokes, Chief Mate;
Lt. H. Kruley; E.P. Rutland,
2nd Engineer; & H.E. Larson,
3rd Engineer. FEB 1943

Captain and crew of a new Liberty Ship [SS Booker T. Washington]
just after it completed its maiden voyage to England.

Picture from Wikipedia User/Haus

Hugh Nathaniel Mulzac was an African-American member of the United States Merchant Marine. He earned a Master rating in 1918 which should have qualified him to command a ship, but this did not happen until September 29, 1942 because of racial discrimination.

Born on March 26, 1886 on Union Island in Saint Vincent and the Grenadines, his life at sea started right after high school when he served on British schooners.

With a mate's license from Swansea Nautical College he rose to the rank of mate before immigrating to the United States in 1918. Within two years he had earned the first ever master's certificate ever issued to an African-American. He served as a mate on the SS *Yarmouth* of the Black Star Line until that line went out of business in 1922.

For the next two decades the only shipboard work Mulzac could get was in the steward's departments on several shipping lines.

Mulzac was finally promoted to the rank of captain, but he refused the offer because the rank was attached to the condition that he would serve above an all-black crew. Mulzac then became a cook for another 22 years.

In 1942 he was offered command of the SS Booker T. Washington, the first Liberty ship to be named after an African-American. He refused at first because the crew was to be all black. He insisted on an integrated crew, stating, "Under no circumstances will I command a Jim Crow vessel." The Merchant Marine finally gave in and agreed to an integrated crew, and he took command from 1942-1947, making 22 round trip voyages and transported over 18,000 soldiers without a single loss of life.

After the war, Mulzac again couldn't get command of a ship. In 1948 he unsuccessfully filed a lawsuit against the ship's operators. In 1950 he made a bid for Queens Borough President under the American Labor Party ticket. He lost the election, having gotten 15,500 votes.

Due to his strong ties to the labor movement, he found himself blacklisted in the era of McCarthyism. At the New York state election, 1958, he ran on the Independent-Socialist ticket for New York State Comptroller.

Mulzac was a self-taught painter, and in 1958, thirty-two of his oil paintings were put on an exhibit at a one man show in the Countee Cullen Library in Manhattan. In 1960 a Federal Judge restored his seaman's papers and license, and at the age of 74 he was able to find work as a night mate.

On September 29, 1920, Hugh Mulzac married Marie Avis, a native of Jamaica; they would have four children. Their youngest daughter, Una Mulzac, was the founder of a prominent Harlem-based political and Black power-oriented bookstore, Liberation Bookstore.

Captain Mulzac died in East Meadow, New York on January 30, 1971.

Torpedo Alley, Wolf Pack, Battle of Midway, Murmansk Run, and Henry Kaiser

When the Japanese attacked Pearl Harbor, the Navy had only a handful of ships and planes to defend the east coast from Maine to Texas. A total armament at the FL Bayport Navy Base was one Browning Automatic Rifle, one Thomson Machine Gun & two 45 Cal. pistols. Shores of the Carolinas were lit up and earned the name "Torpedo Alley." Many armed guards and merchant seamen lost their lives in sight of the American shoreline. In the first seven months of 1942, German subs sank an appalling total of 681 vessels at a very small cost to themselves.

A convoy in 1942, New York to England, was hit by a "wolf pack" of submarines off Cape Farewell, Greenland and lost 22 of 63 ships before the fog blew in and saved the others from annihilation. By far the most hazardous voyage was to Murmansk, North Russia. German occupied Norway allowed their subs, surface craft and aircraft to attack the convoy ships all the way to the city and then bomb them as they waited to unload their needed cargo. Matchless courage and unlimited devotion to duty were unbelievable under such a dreadful situation. Ships leaving ports in the U.S. for Russia had about one chance in three of returning prior to the spring of 1943. Twenty Merchant Ships were sunk at Pearl Harbor. Merchant mariners' casualties were never recorded. The Mariners would have never shipped out again if they had known the devastation that was being done by the enemy. They would have joined the Army or Navy where it was safer.

On June 12, 1942, the Battle of Midway took place at the U.S. small Islands of Midway in the Pacific. Admiral Nimitz's strategy was to use his tactical commanders to bring every naval vessel in the Pacific to Midway for the battle at the same time. The British had decoded the German's military codes without their knowledge. Germany had given those codes to the Japanese. American Intelligence reported these same codes to Nimitz who was known to take a risk. He ordered a careful code message sent out to the Japanese asking their Commanders where their carrier attack force was as well as some details. He was surprised that he got a coded response to everything he asked. Four carriers and hundreds of airmen were lost by the Japanese. The Merchant Marines were there as supporting supply vessels for the naval combatants. One captain said his Liberty ship there was a tanker with a cargo of fuel oil.

The First Liberty Ship

The first Liberty, **S.S. Patrick Henry,** being launched at
Bethlehem-Fairfield shipyard in Baltimore Md. Dec. 1941

Flamboyant, independent **Henry Kaiser**, who helped build the Hoover
Dam, severed his partnership with Todds and became the most famous
shipbuilder of Liberty ships despite his ever having built a ship before.

"Hurry-Up Henry" used mass production methods to build 442-foot vessels at a pace never seen before. Rivets had always been used to hold the steel plates of the hulls together. Kaiser used welding. This was much faster but did not allow the hulls to flex in heavy weather at sea, especially with military overload cargoes. As in every new program there was failure in the welds and some ships broke in half. Henry Kaiser received the brunt of bad publicity at his shipyard in Portland, Oregon. His slower competitors referred to his ships as "Kaiser Coffins." However, there were more Kaiser Liberty ships sunk at sea than from other shipyards because there were more of them in combat. The SS Robert E. Peary was built in four days, fifteen hours and twenty-nine minutes.

The Liberty Fleet

Liberty ships lined up like loaves of bread, as they were
mass produced at the shipyards during the war years.
There were over 2,700 Liberty ships built.

Captain George Duffey and Other Merchant POW Losses

Without protective clothing one can only live in the ocean until hypo-
thermia claims him, and in the North Atlantic that span is a measured
few minutes. When one of our ammunition ships or tankers with aviation
gasoline exploded, there was instant obliteration of men and ship. The
explosion is horrendous as there is a rising cloud of dust and vapor and
nothing falls to earth. The sea is a lethal enemy, boats or not. Our men
were forced by fire to leap into the sea. Young and better swimmers would
look for a life boat, raft or something floating and call out for help which
more often than not will not come. The screaming and yelling of the dying
are remembered for the rest of a survivor's life. And there are sharks in
the ocean. Some of the worst Merchant Marine losses came about during
the Allied invasion of North Africa against German and Italian forces.

On New Year's Day 1943, the SS Arthur Middleton was torpedoed after delivering its cargo of landing-craft tanks. The vessel blew up and broke in half at sea and killed 78 of the 81 men aboard. Only three Naval Armed Guards survived.

A Liberty ship in a Mediterranean convoy was carrying high caliber explosives and 504 U.S. Army Air Force personnel in addition to 47 merchant seamen and 29 from the Navy Armed Guard. On April 20, 1944, German torpedo planes attacked off the coast of Algeria obliterating the ship and killing everyone aboard.

Captain George W. Duffy, then a 3rd officer on the American Leader, a September 1941 graduate of the Massachusetts Nautical School, like Stanley Willner on the M.S. Sawokla, had his ship attacked and sunk a little later by the German Raider "Michel" under the command of Captain Helmuth von Ruckteschell. Twenty-two shipmates were killed. George Duffy was treated well by the Germans on the Michel. But, unlike Stanley Willner and Dennis Roland, he did not work on the Bridge over the River Kwai where hell was at its worst. He was assigned to another work group that was working on another bridge. (Captain Ruckteschell was the only Raider Captain convicted as a war criminal.)

Duffy learned the languages of military men from other nations so that he could communicate with them. His immediate adversaries who did not recognize his officer's status were not the Japanese but were prison British officers. George didn't lose his pride. He said, "Your own men know you are an officer and you are still an American." After his three and a half years as a POW, the war ended. Duffy wasn't lucky like Willner and Roland who got out to an American military hospital and a quick flight toward home. Nobody ever came for him. He and another prisoner took matters into their own hands and started hitchhiking on military aircraft across Asia, North Africa and finally the USA. Years later, a psychiatrist said Duffy had survived because he refused to see himself as a victim.

Captain Duffy earned recognition from his country and has written a book about his WW II experiences, "Ambushed Under the Southern Cross." He tells about his three years as a POW on two German warships and ten labor camps in Java, Singapore and Sumatra in southeast Asia. Duffy's logs while a POW aboard the "Michel," the German vessel that sank the "American Leader," portrays a German Captain who in dealing with the Americans aboard his ship was respectful and humane. He was even sentimental when he delivered the honors at a burial of a crew member of an English ship he sank.

Valor at Sea

On a rainy morning, September 27, 1942, the lookout saw two vessels in the south Atlantic mist heading straight for the SS *Stephen Hopkins*. The *Hopkins* officers quickly determined they were German raiders and a general alarm was sounded. The crew of the approaching cruiser *Stier* had been painting a camouflage on the hull when the raiders came upon what they thought was a setting duck. The *Stier*, with her six 5.9-inch guns, was accompanied by a heavily armed supply ship, the *Tannenfels*.

The Germans opened fire at a range of a thousand yards. One of their salvos hit the main boiler of the Liberty ship, killing men in the engine room and slowing the SS *Stephen Hopkins* to a speed of only one knot. Navy Ensign Ken Willett ran aft and manned the four-inch gun, but shrapnel hit him in the stomach. He kept going until the magazine blew up, killing him. Navy Armed Guard sailors were killed in the forward gun tub. 2nd Mate Joe Layman took their place at the 37mm gun with mess boy Herb Love passing shells to him. They were hitting the *Stier* but the *Tannenfels* fired, killing them both.

Seeing the *Stier* on fire, Capt. Paul Buck brought his ship around so that its aft gun could fire at the *Stier*. The American Liberty ship had been hit many times, was on fire and sinking, but still had some fight left. *Edwin J. O'Hara*, the 18-year-old cadet engineer, helped several injured Navy sailors to safety. Then he ran back to the unmanned aft gun. O'Hara loaded and fired the five remaining shells, hitting the *Stier*. Both German raiders opened fire with their big guns, killing him instantly. A short while later the *Stier* sank, followed by the *Stephen Hopkins* with the Stars and Stripes still flying overhead.

A lifeboat from the ship made its escape across misty, choppy seas, carrying 19 men. Captain Buck was in fact seen on another life raft, but was never heard from again. Four of the men in the lifeboat died before it could eventually make the coast of Brazil a month later, without the aid of navigation instruments or charts.

Some German submarine crews held a high degree of honor and respect for their enemies. This had to do in part with the Germans' awareness that a common fate could await them all. Some of the German submarine crews were bad, but the Japanese were worse because they would fire their machine guns at helpless merchant seamen.

The U.S. Merchant Marine Academy is the only one of the five Federal military academies that send their cadets into combat zones all over the earth. There is a monument on the campus, led by O'Hara's name, with 123 names honoring those young men in officers' training who gave their lives for their country. The large gymnasium is named "O'Hara Hall" where all sorts of functions and entertainment take place.

The SS *Stephen Hopkins* subsequently received the Gallant Ship Award from the War Shipping Administration, one of the few merchant ships to receive a high honor.

Engine Cadet Edwin Joseph O'Hara
(courtesy of www.usmm.org)

Death's Railroad

As Third Mate **Stanley Willner** regained consciousness, the only thing keeping him from drowning was a piece of wreckage he was clinging to. He knew he was somewhere in the Indian Ocean off the coast of Madagascar. He was badly injured. He felt his life force ebbing away and his 22 years flashed before him. He thought of his young pretty wife, Carol. They had kept their May 16, 1942-marriage secret knowing that he would be shipping out very soon and wanted to have a religious ceremony for their parents' sake. Nearby, he could hear others crying out for help, but they were invisible in the dark, choppy and oil-covered seas. After three hours in the water his head throbbed, and there was slight pain in his genitals that became a constant ache.

After graduating from high school in Norfolk, VA in 1938, a neighbor who was aware of his interest of the sea contacted Senator Harry Byrd of Virginia who appointed Stanley Willner as the first Cadet in the U.S. Maritime Service. At that time a few cadets trained for sea duty because the U.S. Merchant Marine Academy had yet to open. He has a three-year training period on several ships and oceans. On August 21, 1942, Stanley was appointed a deck officer with the rank of third mate and an Ensign in the U.S. Naval Reserve. He was proud of the appointments and everything was fine and in "ship shape" until now except for his father having passed away in April the year before.

During WW I, Germany's disguised armed Raiders appearing as harmless merchant ships sank or captured 108 ships. This established a historical precedent for operations in WW II. Only two Raiders in the sea forced the Allies to take action against them. They were a constant worry to the Allies. One of these Raiders was the *Michael*, a converted Polish freighter captured in Danzig and was heavily armed with cannons, machine guns, two scout panes above and below and below water

**Cadet
Stanley Willner**
Officer Willner after graduating from Merchant Marine Academy.

torpedoes. Masts, derricks and her stack were movable to make identification difficult. The diesel engine could provide a 16-knot top speed.

On November 29, 1942, the Army transport M.S. Sawokla, an old freighter owned by American Export lines built in Tampa, Florida in 1920 and refitted in 1927, was headed from Ceylon on a southwesterly course for Cape Town after delivering war materials to the Persian Gulf and Calcutta. Her complement was 41 crew members, 13 Naval Armed Guard and five passengers. The Master was Carl Wink. The Sawokla's cargo was hemp and course canvas bails and 850 tons of diesel fuel. Her light armament was a 4.5 inch cannon and two 22 mm flack cannons on the bridge and two machine guns on the stern.

Willner was straining his eyes looking forward from the bridge into the overcast night when he saw something ahead in the choppy sea. He immediately rang Captain Carl Wink's quarters. At 9:38 p.m., the Michel started firing with her guns and heavy cannon, and the first torpedo was in route. Willner heard the Captain's door close as he was blown overboard. The second heavy artillery barrage struck the engine and radio room. Captain Wink and others on the bridge and radio rooms were killed. There were numerous waterline hits. The Esau raked the deck with machine gun fire. Captain Ruckteschell called cease fire at 9:45 p.m..

The fatal blow occurs when men who were seen running aft caused the German Captain to think they were heading for a cannon on the stern and he ordered another two-minute attack. By that time the jute cargo had ignited and fires began to show on deck. Second Officer Dennis Roland and the survivors abandoned the ship. He and others managed to lower a #two lifeboat but it sank as the air tanks broke loose. That left the men clinging to some oars, afraid to be washed away and afraid of being picked up by the raider lest it is Japanese. When they got a better look at the ship, they all called for help. Roland was not hurt and said he figured it was "nonsense" to die. The second mate on merchant ships is the navigator who sets up the course the ship will follow in its voyage.

Dennis Roland disliked the course they were on because "it was set down the middle of the Indian Ocean in accordance with British Control orders." He would have chosen a course to go between the mainland of Africa and the Island of Madagascar where there was the possibility of air cover and coastal patrol.

At 9:58 the Michel & Esau began their search for survivors. When Stanley Willner was pulled out of the water almost three hours later, he was clinging to a piece of wreckage. Thirty-five survivors were rescued which took three hours with a high speed launch. Fourteen were lost. They were now POWs. Two seriously and seven badly injured men occupied the medical crew under Dr. Schroeder in "sick bay" below. One of them was Stanley Willner. The Esau was the Raiders motor torpedo launch named after the wandering hunter of the Bible.

Willner said the German doctor treated him well, and he received wonderful care and especially his injured leg where the healing was hastened. He was fluoroscoped to find shrapnel fragments in his body. He was operated on at least 10 times. Because of shrapnel his left testicle had to be removed and his penis wounds were treated. After the operation, Dr.Schroder remarked to Willner, "You have the same condition that Hitler has."

25

Willner remembered that he said to himself, "The hell with Adolf Hitler, I just got married."

On one occasion Captain Ruckteschell visited the sick bay and told the POWs that he was not a Nazi and was just doing his duty for his country, and as long as he was Captain the POWs would be treated fairly aboard his ship. He, his officers and crew essentially kept the pledge.

A Christmas 1942 decoration by the Michel's crew was done with whatever they had or could find aboard for the celebration. Dennis Rowland talked to a German Officer about the POWs celebrating Christmas. Officers, men, Americans, British, Greeks and the rest spent the day in the larger crew's quarters. The Germans gave them tiny candles. Rowland said: "It was one of the best Christmas Days I can recall, and it had to be on a German Raider."

On January 8, 1943, Captain von Ruckteschell called the men together to give them the bad news: We are going to Japan . . . and it did not take long for the news to get down to the POWs. Everyone's spirits dropped. No one was going home. The Michel urgently needed repairs, supplies and to send her POWs ashore. She was able to transfer many to German ships at various times. American George Duffy from the sunken American Leader was among the POWs in one of these exchanges. Willner had only been out of the hospital about a week.

After spending nearly a year at sea, the Michel pulled into Batavia on the northwest coast of Java. Afterwards the Germans complained of the discourteous manner in which they were received by their allied Japanese who treated them a little better than spies. No POWs were needed there so they sailed off to Singapore where Stanley Willner and Dennis Roland remained together as they were marched off the ship. When the POWs left the ship it became apparent that the Germans had become attached to them. As scruffy men tramped down the gang plank with their few belongings, more than one German cried openly. Roland had all hands sign a letter of appreciation to them for their humane treatment.

Meanwhile, the U.S. Navy Department's Bureau of Naval Personnel issued a letter to the Secretary of the Navy on February 27, 1943 canceling Ensign Stanley Willner's commission in the USNR. The letter stated that the "Applicant is deceased." Totally in the dark regarding what happened to Willner's ship, his family went into deep shock, especially his wife, Carol. At this point she finally told them she and Stanley were married.

When the Michel arrived in Tokyo in March 1943, Capt. Ruckteschell had become ill. He was suffering from a "tense stomach and a valvular defect" and was relieved of duty. He was sent to a hospital in Peking until the war ended. Helmuth Ruckteschell was the only Raider Capt. to be tried for war crimes by a British Military Court. He was sentenced to 10 years in prison that was reduced to seven years due to his heart defect and died in prison 24 June 1948. The trial left von Ruckteschell a broken man. He told his wife, "I want you to know that my conscience as a human being is clear. So pray for us." One of the POW officers who spent 80 days captive on the Michel said "Ruckteschell was a Christian and a gentleman."

Changi Barracks

The Changi Peninsula was the receiving area for all POWs captured after the fall of Singapore. This little group became a part of the thousands of men from Australian, British and Dutch Armies that fell when the Japanese defeated them at Singapore. On August 30, 1942, before the Michel's POWs arrived here, the Imperial Japanese Army issued a Declaration ordering every prisoner of war to sign it. *I the undersigned solemnly swear on my honor that I will not, under any circumstances, attempt to escape!* The POWs refused to sign the document and the Japs took swift revenge via any and every measure. Eventually Allied Commanders negotiated with the IJA that an actual order be issued to the POW to sign the Declaration.

Their officers pointed out to their troops that unless they did so, large scale epidemics of disease would break out and their deaths were likely. They signed the required Declaration but not until September 5 did the Japs allow them to return to their areas.

During Willner and Rolands march to the Changi Camp they had to pass through Raffels Square, Singapore. A rude shock awaited them. Hanging from several crudely made gallows were naked and decomposed bodies of women. The guards let it be known that these women refused to sleep with Japanese soldiers.

During their first muster before being processed in the POW camp, the British sergeant gave the letter that German Dr. Schroder had written for him to turn over to the Japanese Dr. in the POWs camp. He was still suffering from his near fatal wounds received in the sinking of the Sawokla. The guard tore it to shreds and swung his rifle at Willner knocking him down.

Dazed, bleeding and lying in the dirt, he thought this is not going to be easy, and from that moment on every one of his party knew they were in for a very hard time. Willner and his group settled into the camp routine and were fortunate because their huts were outside the main walls. These huts held 70-80 men each. Sleeping accommodations were on boards and not on the ground. Usually there was one muster per day. Willner worked on the docks unloading ships.

Australian and British troops managed to salvage a lot of their clothing and equipment after they surrendered. This was not the case for the *Michel's POWs*. Willner had no clothing other than what he was wearing when his ship was torpedoed. An Australian gave him a piece of cloth which he fashioned into a "G-string." A G-string was the usual dress for a POW. It was a piece of cloth about three feet long and nine inches wide with a string on one end to use as a belt. Willner had no shoes and was barefoot for his whole captivity with the Japanese. He had a tin can he carried with him all the time.

REMEMBERSINGAPORE.WORDPRESS.com

The CHANGI Barracks Ruins

During this period at Changi, Stanley began collecting drawings, poems, cartoons and other memorabilia that he fashioned into a scrapbook. He used toilet paper for the scrapbook, buried it from time to time to conceal it wrapped in plastic. Discovery would have meant instant death.

Among the POWs, British officers were in command at Chanji. They in turn received their orders from the Japanese and our officers were informed right away that they fell under the command of the British, not what the Japs says. A POW wrote that the camp was run by a typical British officer with a swagger stick and his ribbons and pushy mannerisms. If an American officer wanted to speak to the Japanese or complain about anything, they had to go through the proper chain of command. If the British felt it was warranted, they could do so.

As WW II Mariners, let us recall our view of the British at Changi barracks in Singapore. We could not quite understand why there were more than 50,000 men in the British, Australian and Dutch armies there as POWs who were surrendered by their top commanders at Singapore. We knew about high wartime casualties in combat zones and fighting to your death. Ours were the highest of any service at one in every 16 men. After the two atomic bombs fell on Japan and the war ended, American ships were hurried to Singapore with supplies, food and fuel. The City-State citizens were in terrible shape. I was a 19-year-old Cadet engineer on the SS San Pasqual, a T-2 tanker, and we made three trips from the refinery in Abadan, Iran to Singapore with fuel. The people there had lived in terror of the Japanese occupation, but they put government and all its functions back together along with private enterprise. Entertainment, restaurants, and movies were back in service. And there were many new POWs working on the streets and in the city. Of course we crazy Americans had to see some action, and every night when the city closed down, and after a drink or two, we would contact the ricksha owners for a barefoot race to our dock and make wagers on our man until the Police Chief asked our Captain to please end that disturbance on their streets. We gave them a week's earnings for every race and they praised the Americans.

We learned a lot about the Japanese and that the British had 18 inch cannons pointed out to sea that could not turn backward as the Japs came in the back way because they had only anticipated a naval invasion of Singapore.

Living conditions at Changi were just bearable and the POWs did their best to keep their quarters and surroundings neat and sanitary. However, there were plenty of lice and bed bugs. Cleanliness, or rather the lack of it on the part of some POWs, played an important role in most of the camps in light of the few medical supplies available. Willner's wounds healed in the two months he was incarcerated in Changi. No bandages or medicine was offered. Despite his being an officer, he did not rate favored treatment, especially from the British. Changi Gaol was another

POW camp in the area. Stanley spent some time in the Sime Road Prison before being transported to Changi Gaol where he remained until the war ended.

The question of where to get the manpower became the primary issue. That answer was simple as the Japanese were concerned. As the Jap juggernaut swept through the Far East, hundreds of thousands of Allied personnel and local citizenry of the captured countries were made POWs. It was decided to use POW labor to build the 261-mile railroad. To save time, money and merchant shipping to supply the Japanese army, work began on both ends of the prospective railroad at the same time. Although they did not sign the 1929 Geneva Accords, they voiced their approval and did sign the Hague Conference in 1907 which forbade using POWs as laborers. In April 1942, when the Japanese had acquired 300,000 prisoners of various types, it was decided that all military personnel be made to earn their keep. This huge pool of labor convinced the Japanese authorities that a rail link to Burma was a viable proposition. The men of the Rising Sun believed they were honoring the dishonorable by allowing their defeated foes to work on a project sanctioned by the Emperor.

> **This fateful decision resulted in more than 300,000 men being involved in building a railroad. Seventy thousand were POWs.**
>
> **16,000 died.**
>
> **700 were Americans.**

The Burma-Siam Railroad

It is known less for its physical characteristics than for its association with the monumental struggle which took place along the eastern bank in 1942 & 1943, as a third of a million men strove to build a railway linking Thailand with Burma. Its gruesome notoriety did not come from it being a remarkable engineering achievement. Time was of the element and the railway along the Kwai was built like the pyramids of old, with the labor and lives of a multitude.

The bridge over the River Kwai as it looks today

In January 1942, Japan formed an alliance with Thailand allowing for the capture of Burma and Malaya. By the end of June 1943, all of Burma and the Malay Peninsula were in their possession south to Singapore. Japan had an urgent need for fuel and lubricant oil back at the homeland to supply their war machine. Their sources were minimal. Capture of the oil fields was the first objective, but the Japs did not have a fleet of tankers to carry the crude oil to their refineries. By the end of

1942, the Japanese had lost more than 240 merchant ships. For all their initial successes they did not learn how to form effective, sophisticated, escorted convoy systems with air support as did the U.S. and their allies in the north Atlantic. And they could not quickly build ships to cover their losses.

Having so quickly conquered so much territory, Japan had to supply its far-flung troops which meant creating a logistical supply line from the homeland to the newly conquered areas such as Burma. They depended upon free movement in the Andaman Sea and control of the facilities at the Rangoon docks in order to operate the 30,000 to 40,000 tons of shipping which were needed to make the trip to the main port of Burma each week if their forces were kept supplied. Transport of goods to Burma was through the China Sea around Singapore, through the Strait of Malacca into the Andaman Sea and finally Rangoon. If Bangkok could be used as a railroad transport facility, more than 1,000 miles of this route and the vulnerability of Japanese supply ships to Allied attack could be eliminated.

In the late 19th century, the British developed a plan to link Rangoon with Bangkok, but the projected cost and time involved prevented them from undertaking the project. Although the route was feasible, Japanese engineers thought it would take five or six years.

"H" Force

"H" Force was the group Stanley was assigned to in working on the railroad. Willner made quite a few friends among the POWs. One was British Lt. Earnest Gordon who after the war became a Presbyterian Minister and eventually served as Dean of the Chapel & Divinity at Princeton University from 1955 to 1981. Reverend Gordon very adequately described the Japanese in his book in two sentences: *During the four years they were in control, the Japanese military violated every civilized code. They murdered prisoners by bayoneting, shooting, drowning, or decapitation: they murdered them covertly by working them beyond human endurance, torturing them and denying them medical care.*

A half a world away in New York the Willner family received an official letter from the Director of Naval Personnel in NY City, dated March 5, 1943, stating that Stanley Willner was deceased. Stanley's wife filed for the insurance claim to which she was entitled under the Social Security Act. She received a letter dated July 8, 1943 stating that she was entitled to a mere $190.68. She was also informed that because of her brief marriage before his death, she would not be able to collect monthly benefits once she reached the age of 65.

Not having any concrete evidence of where or when Stanley died or was killed, his wife Carol clung to the hope that he was still alive. A few days after receiving the insurance letter that hope was validated when the International Red Cross delivered a post card that Stanley had written. Having a letter written in her husband's handwriting saying he was alive, she said was like receiving words direct from God.

The post card was followed by a letter from the Prisoners of War Information Bureau documenting Japan's ease of restrictions on POW aid. The Willners then sent weekly packages to Stanley and the other POWs. Carol's uncle was a pharmacist and he gave her a bottle of vitamins to send. Stanley said the vitamins were the only items he ever received. "The Japs took everything else." After the war, Carol found out that Stanley would bury the vitamins and dole them out to the sickest POWs. She quit her job in NYC and moved down to live with Stanley's mother in Norfolk, VA who had a store. She helped her mother-in-law and cried her-self to sleep every night worrying about Stanley ever making it back alive. His mother would not sell nylon hose to civilians. When a sailor came in for nylon hose for his wife or girlfriend, she would not sell the hose to him; she gave him the hose.

Work force "H" was the second group created that spring and was sent to work on the railroad in May 1943 and initially the Japanese wanted the railroad finished by the end of the month. When it became apparent that they would not reach that goal, a new decree was issued. The "Speedo" phase Construction was to be hastened at all costs. Thailand was to supply workers for the railroad, but Thias and Burmese are agricultural people and know nothing about the severe manual labor on such a project. Then the monsoons began early that spring. Confronted with these bad conditions the Imperial General Headquarters at last postponed the target for two months.

The Railway Corps requested an additional 3,300 men to work the difficult mid-section of the rail line where cuttings and tunnels had to be blasted through the mountains. The "H" force group worked the hardest and suffered the second highest death rate, much of which was due to the treatment the POWs endured. They were never transferred from the Singapore to the Thailand Japanese Command where they were looked upon as Singapore's responsibility.

Early in the morning of May 4 Willner was awakened by the commotion going on outside his hut. The Japs were combing the camp for men to add to the "H" force. Stanley Willner, Dennis Roland and the other five Merchant Mariners from the torpedoed Sawokla were in the group known as H6, which was about 100 strong. Willner said they were taken to small flat metal cars riding on a narrow gauge railway and packed in like sardines. The train stopped only once on the first day about noon near a pineapple field. A lot of the pineapples eaten by the men were rotten which caused many cases of diarrhea in those packed cars. You just let go where you were standing. After a few days the cars smelled like sewer barges.

In those five hideous days and nights, Chaplain L. Marsden said he thought they only stopped for food six times in which they were given containers of cold rice and a small piece of fish. They were given 20 minutes to get the food, eat it and return the container. Korean Guards with fixed bayonets were stationed at the front and rear of the marching column. The Japanese would not allow any men to be left behind. They arrived at Ban Pong at 3:00 A.M. of the sixth and were marched to the transit camp a mile from the station. None of the units passing through had any time to exercise hygiene control, and the whole camp was an accumulation of filth as was the dirt floored Convalescent Camp. For many it was a death sentence.

If you were walking along, you would have to yell and salute at the same time to a Japanese officer. If you did not do it loud or fast enough, they would hit you with a rifle butt and then kick you. Stanley says they would treat you like a cockroach running across the kitchen floor. The Korean guards were even meaner than the Japs, as they were forced laborers working as prison guards. The Japs beat up on the POWs and Koreans, and they took it out on us.

Willner, on elephant riding detail, was able to "filch" a duck one day and gave it to the one-legged Englishman the Jap officer had thrown into a boiling bath tub to keep it for him. The Jap officers thought it belonged to one of their officers. The POWs discovered that if they fed the duck several snails a day, it would lay an egg. This would help save US Merchant Marine officer Dennis Roland's life. Dennis took very good care of his men, shielding them as much as he could, but one day he came down with appendicitis and had an emergency appendectomy.

The operation was performed by a Dutch hypnotist who put Dennis into a trance. The doctor sutured him up with the only thread available – canvas thread. Lt. Dennis Roland was able to recover with the aid of duck eggs for food and pulverized shell for vitamins. They usually had only one meal a day which was watery stew with a big spoonful of rice and a pint of boiled water. The rice always had insects in it which were eaten for their protein value. You ate anything you could possibly eat to survive – bugs, dogs, leaves, mice, rats, snails, snakes. You ate your meal when the Japs felt like feeding you. There was very little hygiene in the camps. You were just too exhausted to give a damn.

The Japanese were demanding the POWs work longer and harder. They decided to work day and night. Continuous rain with mud and slush everywhere was making conditions in the camps worse than ever before. The outbreak of cholera was inevitable, and the POWs were told repeatedly: "Don't drink anything but boiled water." But the heat and working conditions drove many of the POWs insane, and the desire for any water to bathe in or drink became a problem. The number of sick continued. On June 16, 1943, the first cholera death occurred among the POWs.

They began dropping like flies according to Willner. The Japs didn't care. All they wanted was to finish the railroad. They had no medication for their own troops, let alone for the POWs. It seemed they were losing almost two dozen POWs a day. What the Japanese did insist upon was the burning of the victims. They were terribly afraid of catching the disease. It was the worst experience as a POW for Stanley. He was called upon by the British, who hated to bury their own, to join about 25 men whose responsibility was to build a big wood fire and throw the cholera victims into the flames, including those who had not died yet. They were forced to do it, and Stanley has never forgotten the odor of 200 burials as he approaches 90 years of age. Chaplain Marsden officiated at many of these burials.

The railway was completed on October 25, 1943. What was left of "H" Force and Willner's group was removed from the area and sent south to recover. After recovery, they were to be sent to Japan for further work. The Japanese began to make arrangements to transfer 10,000 of the Thailand-based prisoners to Japan to work in the heavy industries there. The labor shortage in the homeland was now so acute. This plan never material-ized because for all intents and purposes the "H" force had been worked to death. Chaplain Marsden said: "The men of the "H" force, however, having had the heart worked out of them by slave conditions, were just discarded and left to die."

"Wreckages of Humanity"

The fittest of the prisoners represented a very valuable supplement to what was available, if only the means could be found for transporting them to Japan. Those POWs did not look like men, but were not quite animals. Their feet were covered by bamboo thorns after working long months without boots. Their shins had no flesh, and their blackened calves had holes and bumps. Their thigh and pelvic bones stood out sharply and at the point of each thigh bone was a red, raw patch like a monkey's behind. All their ribs showed clearly.

Arms hung down stick-like with huge hands, wrinkled like old men where the muscle had vanished. Heads were shrunken into skulls with large teeth and faintly glowing eyes set back in wells. Their hair was matted and life-less. The whole body was draped with a loose-fitting envelope of thin brown parchment. Their buttocks were fleshless.

Prisoners from Japanese prison camp

Some of them worked on the famous bridge over the River Kwai

Once the railway was completed, the Japanese Malayan Administration began to withdraw the shattered "F" and "H" Forces back to their bases in Singapore. By December 22, 1943, all of the "F" and "H" Forces except 700 very sick patients at Kanchanaburi Hospital had returned to Singapore. Stanley Willner was in bad condition and his weight had dropped to about 80 pounds or less. He was a small man and did not shave while he worked on the railroad. John Wisecup, a tough U.S. Marine who knew Willner and Dennis Roland, said food was always foremost in the POWs' thoughts. Stanley looked like a younger version of Abe Lincoln. John was considered a "tough guy" when he survived maggots in his leg ulcers. He said he was just lucky. Conditions at these makeshift hospitals were appalling. Willner was fortunate to be treated by an Australian dentist who performed dental "magic" with an old foot-pedal powered dental drill. Some cavities were filled.

Life was easier at these convalescent camps where there was a thriving black market with the Thai natives. Dennis Roland was an officer and was good at trading where anything and everything were traded for food. He would go outside the wire barrier to barter and smuggle for food for his men. Had he ever been caught, it would have been the end of him and every one of his men. According to Stanley, the camps always had one or two "comfort women" – none of whom were pretty. They were subject to the Japanese sexual desires where they would line up by rank to have their needs taken care of.

Willner said the Japs took particular delight in telling POWs that land plots had been mapped out in Malaysia for the POWs to live and work on once the war had been won by the Japanese. They instilled the fear of reprisal against the POWs should the Allied forces invade the area or Japan. The POWs lives would be on the line, and instant death would be the suitable recourse within hours should an invasion occur. This was a real and constant fear since the Allies were already bombing the railroad line, and the Americans were planning to bomb the homeland.

Dennis Roland was asked by the small group of survivors from the U.S. 131st Field Artillery and the sunken USS Huston to be their officer since they did not have one, and he accepted. The Americans were billeted in a former garage with a group of Australians. They stated that Roland as Commander and Willner were billeted with the English officers. They worked together to help us get a fair shake on rations, etc. The British would short change us at every opportunity. Roland was a gamecock and went to bat for us daily. Things were looking better for "H" Force survivors in December 1943. They were shipped to Camp Sime Road that had been British HQ at the beginning of the war. Chaplain Marsden, with the help of a few sympathetic Catholic soldiers, was able to build a little chapel there.

Many of the POWs began to recover physically, but very slowly, while others just gave up the will to live and died. For the survivors the psychological recovery would take much longer and take many years after the war ended. For some the mental process has lasted a lifetime.

Changi Gaol – Spring 1944 to August 1945

Early in 1944, the Japs decided to consolidate the prisoners at Sime Road and other camps to Changi Gaol where Singapore civilians served their time. Construction began in 1932 and accommodation was for 568 inmates on 13 acres of land. Over the years several extensions and changes had been made. The Japanese crowded 10,000 to 15,000 within these maximum security walls before the war ended. At times more than 50,000 POWs and civilians were incarcerated there. So, once again the POWs have to build their own camp and facilities around the walls of the prison. Materials were the only thing supplied by their captors. The jail was not in operable condition when the POWs arrived. No steam kitchen was supplied by oil-burning boilers. No oil.

Upon their arrival, Willner, Roland and a dozen other men crowded into a jail cell which was supposed to hold only one prisoner. It wasn't long before "tough" U.S. Marine John Wisecup got himself into trouble with the prison command again. He, a British cook and two others got caught stealing rice. Although not court marshaled by the British, he was put on the top floor of the jail in isolation for two weeks. After his release, here's what he had to say: "I'll never forget a favor those two guys did for me. When I got out of solitary for stealing that rice on a working party, I went over to the officers lines to scrounge some chow. Dennis and Stanley fixed me up a good meal. I ain't likely ever to forget that. We were on starvation rations over at our hut back of the wall. There can't be hardly anything worse than hunger."

Ronald Searle was making a miraculous recovery at Sime Road and was soon well enough to commence drawing again. He was a close friend of Willner. (Searle was a British cartoonist who was sent to Singapore in January 1942, and was captured when the Japanese invaded. Nothing more was heard of him for almost two years. Searle kept busy involving himself in POW theatrical productions, and he helped with a POW newspaper. Besides irritating the British camp officers, he annoyed the camp clergy and shortly afterwards found himself working on the Railroad.) Searle got his theater up and running, and Stanley and Dennis played two or more roles in one of his productions in the summer of 1944. Theatrical productions were good for the POWs' morale, but the long days' work and terrible living conditions remained with them. It also became dangerous to work outside as the Allies began to bomb Japan fortifications at Singapore.

As Christmas approached in 1944, a few Red Cross parcels made it to Changi Gaol. Willner and others were trying to get off a telegram to their families. Though strictly censored it was a direct line to loved ones back home. Christmas, 1944, was a sad time for the POWs. Christmas dinner amongst Ron Searle's friends consisted of three kittens eaten as holiday fare. Those POWs had to kill and eat any animal they could find and catch to stay alive. Many of them starved anyway.

As the war dragged on into 1945, the economic noose around Japan's neck tightened. Food rations dwindled further as our Allies bombed dock and railroad facilities preventing imports. Of the 11 ounces of food the Japs allowed per man per day, two-thirds was rice, a limited nutrient. The extra portion distributed on April 29, the Emperor's birthday, did nothing to help the men's despondency. Beriberi was present. U.S. Marine John Wisecup remembered: "The last six months at Changi were murder." His size 14 feet looked like basketballs. He had no shoes for two years.

Adolph Hitler's death on April 30, 1945 and the surrender of the Third Reich on May 7 were bad omens for the Japanese. With the food supplies dwindling and Singapore being bombed, panic began to set in, and the Japanese increased the work load. But how much can be gotten from a beaten body? They began to prepare Singapore for the possibility of an Allied attack. Moats, high embankments, barbed-wire fences, caves, tunnels and many other defense measures were quickly taken. At the headquarters of Field Marshal Count Terauchi, commander of the Southern Army in Singapore, plans were being made to kill all prisoners if an attack was made. This was learned from the Korean guards, natives and other sources.

Chaplain Marsden: By April 1945, thousands of men were taken away from the camp to prepare battle stations as a final stand to retain the island fortress. From April until August, when the surrender came, I saw men working from 10 to 12 hours on a few ounces of rice and a little dried white bait.

POW Russell Braddon: When each air raid came, the Nip Air Force fled until the All Clear Sounded. But that did not save their shipping in the docks from destruction.

It took months to repatriate all the POWs from the Singapore area. By May 1946, the number was 96,500. Willner was released as a POW on

September 9, 1945. Stanley Willner and Dennis Roland were fortunate to leave in early September. A letter dated September 10 was sent to Willner's wife stating that he had arrived safely in Calcutta. He was suffering from beriberi, scurvy, dysentery, malaria, fungus, sores etc. He looked like a walking corpse. Upon arrival in early morning at the 142nd U.S. Army Hospital, the former POWs were quickly attended to. Stanley weighed about 75 pounds. His condition was so bad that the doctor who first saw him broke down and cried.

Their first night in the hospital they did not feel clean enough to sleep on those white sheets on the beds and slept on the floors. As they convalesced, the reality of their situation became more apparent. Willner and Roland were in the US Maritime Service. Despite being sworn in as officers of the US Naval Reserve, those who served in the US Merchant Marine were not considered part of the armed services. As a result they were shunned by the military authorities and denied the benefits given to the other military services.

Upon my appointment as a Cadet Midshipman, Engineer, I was sworn into the US Naval Reserve before reporting to the Merchant Marine Cadet Corps initial basic training facility at Pass Christian, MS. After four months of intensive basic marine engineering and gunnery training in class, I was sent to ports for assignment to a merchant ship. When on those orders, we traveled and resided in the port city at our own expense. I had to travel from New Orleans to New York with a week's stop at my home near Kingsport, TN. Being in uniform and training as an officer and a gentleman, it was gratifying to see the number of civilians who wanted to help us by giving us a ride, a meal and good, cheap place to reside in at night. There was a quiet "weed 'em out" practice to determine the most likely officers' material among us. Those dismissed then had to face their draft committee when they got home.

A Merchant Mariner is on his own financially when off his ship.

Recovery

Stanley Willner flew from New York City to Washington, D.C.. Carol Willner had taken the train to D. C. to meet him. "I ran right past him and he caught me," Carol said. "Never would I have recognized this skeleton of a man with sunken eyes that were black down to his cheeks."

Various physicians are recorded in the health study of WW II POWs. One doctor stated, "It's my opinion that virtually none of the prisoners of war of the Japanese who underwent internment for three to 3.5 years escaped without some impairment of their health."

Following the trauma of battle was the shock of capture.

1. They had to adapt to a completely different way of life, deprived of freedom for an indefinite period, cut off from all sources of news and little, if any, mail from home.
2. They lived under appalling conditions, often working very long hours, doing very arduous and often hazardous work while suffering from starvation and malnutrition as well as chronic and recurrent disease.
3. There were the ever present language and culture problems, and the prisoners were at the mercy of cruel, vindictive and unpredictable guards.
4. There was no leave, and they were in contact with the enemy 24 hours a day, seven days a week for years.
5. They were again subjected to the pressure of battle when bombed and strafed by their own people.
6. After repatriation, there was the tremendous shock of adapting to a way of life that had changed greatly during the period of their captivity.

While living in Norfolk, VA, Willner's health deteriorated to the point he went to the Marine Hospital for treatment. Two weeks was all the medical time the Government gave him. They did not know what to do for him. It was over a year and a half before he could return to work. During that period he suffered from a number of illnesses besides waking up nightly in a sweat, screaming from nightmares and blacking out if he tried to walk. According to his wife, he had a ringworm that covered half of his stomach which he couldn't get rid of by any medical treatment. Finally, he got in touch with a British doctor, Dr. Philips, whom he knew as a POW, who sent him some medicine. It worked.

Willner worked part time for the Maritime Commission selling their surplus ships to foreign governments. At lunch time one day he was doing an inspection on a ship when one of the workers picked up and fired a torch. This caused a piece of slag to hit the railing and hit him in the eye, and they could not save it. On the operating table he called Carol to make sure she would not lose the baby she was carrying. They had a fat, baby boy whom they named Mark. Four years after Mark was born, they had a daughter named Nan.

Dennis Roland took a year to recover from his POW ordeals. He and Stanley Willner visited each other and were close friends until Dennis passed away. Roland went on active duty in the Navy in 1947, served in the Korean War, spent eight years in the service and retired as a Lt. Commander. Then he went back to work for American Export Lines. Willner and Roland participated in two major POW reunions and a few others over the years. Stan and Rollie attended a POW reunion at the infamous Bridge over the River Kwai known as *The March of Forgiveness* after disagreeing on this trip. While Roland viewed the walk across the bridge as a gesture to forgive and forget the harshness and deaths, Stanley refused to march across with his dear friend and watched from a distance saying, *"I Can't Forget or Forgive."*

Japanese War Crimes

Japanese war crimes occurred during the period of Japanese imperialism, primarily during the Second Sino-Japanese War and World War II. Some of the incidents have also been described as an Asian Holocaust and Japanese war atrocities. Some war crimes were committed by military personnel from the Empire of Japan in the late 19th century, although most took place during the last part of the *Showa Era*, the name given to the reign of Emperor Hirohito, until the military defeat of the Empire of Japan, in 1945.

Historians and governments of some countries hold Japanese military forces, namely the Imperial Japanese Army, the Imperial Japanese Navy and the Imperial Japanese family, especially Emperor Hirohito, responsible for killings and other crimes committed against millions of civilians and prisoners of war. Some Japanese soldiers have admitted to committing these crimes.

Since the 1950s, senior Japanese Government officials have issued numerous apologies for the country's war crimes. Japan's Ministry of Foreign Affairs states that the country acknowledges its role in causing "tremendous damage and suffering" during World War II, especially in regard to the IJA entrance into Nanjing during which Japanese soldiers killed a large number of noncombatants and engaged in looting. Some members of the Liberal Democratic Party in the Japanese government such as former prime ministers Junichiro Koizumi and Shinzo Abe have prayed at the Yasukuni Shrine, which includes convicted Class A war criminals in its honored war dead. Some Japanese history textbooks only offer brief references to the various war crimes, and members of the Liberal Democratic Party such as Shinzo Abe have denied some of the atrocities such as the use of comfort women.

Crimes

The Japanese military during the 1930s and 1940s is often compared to the military of Nazi Germany during 1933-45 because of the sheer scale of suffering. Much of the controversy regarding Japan's role in World War II revolves around the death rates of prisoners of war and civilians under Japanese occupation. The historian *Chalmers Johnson* has written that:

> "It may be pointless to try to establish which World War Two Axis aggressor, Germany or Japan, was the more brutal to the peoples it victimized. The Germans killed six million Jews and 20 million Russians [i.e., Soviet citizens]; the Japanese slaughtered as many as 30 million Filipinos, Malays, Vietnamese, Cambodians, Indonesians and Burmese, at least 23 million of them ethnic Chinese. Both nations looted the countries they conquered on a monumental scale, though Japan plundered more, over a longer period, than the Nazis. Both conquerors enslaved millions and exploited them as forced laborers – and, in the case of the Japanese, as [forced] prostitutes for front-line troops. If you were a Nazi prisoner of war from Britain, America, Australia, New Zealand or Canada (but not Russia) you faced a 4% chance of not surviving the war; [by comparison] the death rate for Allied POWs held by the Japanese was nearly 30%.

> "According to the findings of the Tokyo Tribunal, the death rate among POWs from Asian countries held by Japan was 27.1%. The death rate of Chinese POWs was much higher because – under a directive ratified on August 5, 1937 by Emperor Hirohito – the constraints of international law on treatment of those prisoners were removed. Only 56 Chinese POWs were released after the surrender of Japan. After March 20, 1943, the Japanese Navy was under orders to execute all prisoners taken at sea."

Cannibalism

Many written reports and testimonies collected by the Australian War Crimes Section of the Tokyo tribunal, and investigated by prosecutor William Webb (the future Judge-in-Chief), indicated that Japanese personnel in many parts of Asia and the Pacific committed acts of cannibalism against Allied prisoners of war. In many cases this was inspired by ever-increasing Allied attacks on Japanese supply lines, and the death and illness of Japanese personnel as a result of hunger. However, according to historian Yuki Tanaka: "Cannibalism was often a systematic activity conducted by whole squads and under the command of officers." This frequently involved murder for the purpose of securing bodies.

For example, an Indian POW, Havildar Changdi Ram, testified that:

> "[On November 12, 1944] the Kempeitai beheaded an [Allied] pilot. I saw this from behind a tree and watched some of the Japanese cut flesh from his arms, legs, hips, buttocks and carry it off to their quarters . . . They cut it [into] small pieces and fried it."

In some cases, flesh was cut from living people. Another Indian POW, Lance Naik Hatam Ali (later a citizen of Pakistan) testified that in New Guinea:

> The Japanese started selecting prisoners and every day one prisoner was taken out and killed and eaten by the soldiers. I personally saw this happen and about 100 prisoners were eaten at this place by the Japanese. The remainder of us was taken to another spot 50 miles [80 km] away where 10 prisoners died of sickness. At this place, the Japanese again started selecting prisoners to eat. Those selected were taken to a hut where their flesh was cut from their bodies while they were alive and they were thrown into a ditch where they later died.

Fight for Veterans' Benefits

The importance of the Merchant Marine contribution to a U.S. victory cannot be overstated. Without their participation in delivering the supplies needed to carry the war to our deadly enemies, we and our Allies would almost certainly have lost WW II.

General Dwight Eisenhower: "On behalf of the men in my command, I thank the men of the Merchant Marine for their pledge of full cooperation in our common effort to destroy the forces of tyranny and darkness. The huge quantities of supplies that have been brought across the Atlantic are a testimonial to the job that has already been done. Every man in this allied command is quick to express his admiration for the loyalty, courage and fortitude of the officers and men of the Merchant Marine. We count upon their efficiency and their utter devotion to duty as we do upon our own. They have never failed us yet, and in all the struggles yet to come we know they will never be deterred by danger, hardship or privation. When final victory is ours, there is no organization that will share its credit more deservedly than the Merchant Marine."

General Douglas MacArthur: "I wish to commend to you the valor of the merchant seamen participating with us in the liberation of the Philippines. With us they have shared the heaviest enemy fire. On this island I have ordered them off their ships and into fox holes when their ships became untenable targets of attack. At our side they have suffered in bloodshed and in death. The caliber of efficiency and the courage they displayed in their part of the invasion of the Philippines marked their conduct throughout the entire campaign in the southwest Pacific area. They have contributed tremendously to our success. I hold no branch in higher esteem than the Merchant Marine." (Press Release, October 14, 1945) "They have brought us our lifeblood and paid for it with some of their own. I saw them bombed off the Philippines and in New Guinea ports. When it was humanely possible, when their ships were not blown out from under them by bombs and torpedoes, they have delivered their cargoes to us who needed them so badly. In war it is performance that counts."

Harry S. Truman, 1951: "During the black years of the war, the men of the Merchant Marine did their job with boldness and daring. Over 6,000 were killed. Many more were missing in carrying out their duties. In memory of those men and in the interest of our Nation, the United States must carry out the bold and daring plan of Franklin D. Roosevelt for a Merchant Marine of the best designed and equipped passenger and cargo ships, manned by the best trained men in the world."

Admiral Chester Nimitz (April 23, 1944): *"The Merchant Marine Service has repeatedly proven its right to be considered as an integral part of our fighting team. Its efforts have contributed in great part to our success. Well done. The United States Merchant Marine played an important part in the achievement of victory in Europe, and is destined to play an even more important role in helping finish off the Japanese. To move great quantities of war materials from principal sources of supply across 6,000 miles of ocean to battle fronts in the Far East is the formidable task now confronting our merchant fleet. We are confident it will be done quickly and efficiently in keeping with the high standards of accomplishment set by the Merchant Marine in every war in our history."*

General George Marshall: (Press Release, May 18, 1945) *"The men and ships of the Merchant Marine have carried out its war mission with great distinction, and have demonstrated its ability to meet the challenges of redeploying our full power for the Pacific."*

Lt. General Alexander Vandergrift, U.S. Marine Corps Commandant: *"The men and ships of the Merchant Marine have participated in every landing of the United States Marine Corps from Guadalcanal to Iwo Jima—and we know they will be at hand with supplies and equipment when American amphibious forces hit the beaches of Japan itself."*

President Franklin D. Roosevelt, 1943: *"The men of our American Merchant Marine have pushed through despite the perils of the submarine, the dive bomber and the surface raider. They have returned voluntarily to their job at sea again and again because they realized that the lifelines to our battle fronts would be broken if they did not carry out their vital part in this global war . . . In their hands our vital supply lines are expanding. Their skill and determination will keep open the highway to victory and unconditional surrender."*

One of President Franklin D. Roosevelt's last public statements on the U.S. Merchant Marine on September 19, 1944 was: *"It seems to me particularly appropriate that Victory Fleet Day this year should honor the men and management of the American Merchant Marine. The operators in this war have written one of its most brilliant chapters. They have delivered the goods when and where needed in every theater of operations and across every ocean in the biggest, the most difficult and dangerous transportation job ever undertaken. As time goes on, there will be greater public understanding of our merchant fleet's record during this war."*

President Franklin D. Roosevelt, during signing of the GI Bill on June 22, 1944, stated: *"I trust Congress will soon provide similar opportunities to members of the Merchant Marines who have risked their lives time and time again during war for the welfare of their country."*

President Roosevelt died in Warm Springs, Georgia on April 12, 1945, and our Merchant Marine opportunity for recognition and any benefits at all died with him.

Nearly 7,300 mariners were killed at sea. 12,000 were wounded, and at least 1,100 of these died as a result of their wounds. Six hundred and sixty-three men and women were taken prisoners. Some were blown to death, some incinerated, some drowned, some froze, some starved, and 66 died in prison camps or aboard Japanese ships while being transported to other prison camps. Thirty-one ships vanished without a trace to a watery grave.

One in 26 mariners serving aboard merchant ships during WW II died in the line of duty. The Merchant Marine suffered a greater percentage of war-related deaths than all other U. S. services. Casualties of men and ships were not recorded to keep the enemy unaware of their successes and also to attract and keep mariners at sea. The average in 1942 was 33 Allied ships each week. A series of sealed orders was given to the Captain on setting his course. Even after the war ended, merchant seamen, unlike those in the Armed Services, couldn't go home. The WSA, War Shipping Administration, stated: Men are still needed to man merchant ships in excess of those presently available and will be needed for some months to come. Millions of our Armed Forces must be brought home, and supplies must be carried to the occupations forces throughout the world. Supplies must also be carried for the rehabilitation of devastated areas.

When the war ended, we were discharging fuel from our tanker in Aden, Yemen. We cadet engineers were awakened by all kinds of loud noises on shore and in the city as everyone seemed to be celebrating the situation. I recall our thinking that our ship could turn north on the Red Sea, pass through the Suez Canal into the Mediterranean and out into the Atlantic and back to the USA. Our Captain received an order signed by President Harry Truman that the SS San Pasqual would remain on our assigned route of loading oil cargoes at the refinery at Abadan, Iran and making the shuttle runs to Aden and going to Indonesia and Australia as well. The war ended August 15, 1945. After having to go to Venezuela, we did not get to Baltimore until May 21, 1946. Then we were ordered to go to New York and take an exam on what we had learned at sea before heading home.

Some Merchant Mariners were actually entitled to veteran benefits under an old law of the U.S. Code (46 U.S. C. 225), dated May 28, 1896, which stated:

Service During War – No master, mate, pilot or engineer of steam vessels licensed under Title L II (R.S. 4399-4500) of the Revised Statutes shall be liable to draft in time of war, except for the performance of duties such as required by his license; while performing such duties in the service of the United States every such master, mate, pilot or engineer shall be entitled to the highest rate of wages paid by the Merchant Marine of the United States for similar services; and if killed or wounded while performing such duties under the United States, they or their heirs or legal representatives shall be entitled to all privileges accorded to soldiers and sailors serving the Army or Navy under the pension laws of the United States.

Lewis B. Hershey, director of the Selective Service Administration, decided to suspend this statute during the war and supersede it with the provision of the 1940 Selective Service Act. Captain Warren G. Leback said the merchant seamen were "fighting the war" when these political machinations occurred. A few expletives could be expected when Hershey's name was spoken.

In the poisoned atmosphere at the conclusion of WW II, anti-Merchant Marine lobbying intensified despite their wartime suffering. Communists had been involved in the American labor movement in the 1930s. The old accusation that the seaman's unions were run by Communists resurfaced though their influence by wartime had proved insignificant. Our Seaman's Bill of Rights crashed on the rocks in 1947. The House Un-American Activities Committee claimed our Radio Operators Unions were Communistic. Radio officers were often the most heroic of Merchant Mariners, staying on board their sinking ship after enemy attack to continue distress messages. The enemy knew that and tried to kill the radio officer quickly just as they tried to torpedo the engine room to kill the engineers, destroy the engines and stop the ship for the kill.

Congress put a stripped-down package of benefits in the Seamen's Bill of Rights through the legislative motions in 1947, but it died in a committee without Roosevelt. At "The Big Three" Tehran Summit Conference of Joseph Stalin, Franklin D. Roosevelt and Winston Churchill on November 28 to December 1, 1943, they concluded that they could win WW II by opening a massive front in Europe on Nazi Germany by May 1, 1944.

Why did President Roosevelt sign the "GI Bill of Rights" on June 1, 1944 giving military veterans education and training for jobs, generous loan provisions (for homes, farms and businesses) mustering-out pay and unemployment compensation? Our Navy Armed Guards that sailed with us Merchant Mariners on our ships were eligible and deserving. In contrast, the merchant seaman received nothing beyond a worthless paper discharge certificate. However, thousands of veterans who had spent three or four years at their desks all over the country welcomed the Serviceman's Readjustment Act of 1944 (GIBR)

Franklin D. Roosevelt served as Assistant Secretary of the Navy, 1913-18, which included all of the United States participation in WW I. In 1932, in the midst of the "Great Depression," the veterans of WW I asked for the bonus Congress had set aside for them to be paid in 1950. It was a sort of a life insurance bill. The hearing and the proposed bill didn't make it to a bonus, and some 20,000-25,000 angry, hungry and unemployed veterans descended on Washington, D.C. They set up camps in the city parks and huge park near the Capitol "on the hill." Nothing happened and they became a bit unruly. The city and federal authorities ordered their police forces to drive the vets out of town. They were no match for the veterans who were running the cops out of town. Then the Army, under Col. Douglas MacArthur, ran the vets out of Washington with tanks and tear gas. That news quickly passed all over the country, and the Washington brass was in deep trouble with relatives, friends and families of these men who fought and won WW I. The vets went home but kept a four-year pressure on their Congressmen and Senators until they got their bonuses in 1936. I was ten years old when my Dad, who had inhaled mustard gas while on military guard duty, received his bonus which was around $300, as I recall, and that was quite a bit of money in those times.

Ailing President Franklin D. Roosevelt and a few elderly Congressmen and Senators clearly recalled to mind the 1932 march on Washington. They said, "What can we do when we have to bring back 12 to 15 million veterans to the United States?" They passed the GI Bill, and it worked for all vets unless you were a merchant seaman like me and many other grads of the US Merchant Marine Academy and the State Academies who were sworn in Deck and Engineering Naval Reserve Officers.

Stormy Waters

In the spring of 1942, the U.S. Navy attempted to take control of the Merchant Marine. To justify this move they charged that "there has been a failure by cargo vessel crews and officers to obey Navy orders and . . . the discipline of the crews afloat and ashore is inadequate." With the assistance of the unions, the merchant shipping thwarted this attempt, thus protecting their lucrative government contracts. The unions representing seamen thought that their interest and those of the companies were parallel. But, they were shortsighted in accepting increased wages for membership. It cost them the extensive benefits of the G.I. Bill after the war, and it turned out even worse. They received no medical coverage, and the increased wages they were receiving were really not higher at all as a comparison in this book will show.

It was a severe, critical, strategic, political mistake for the unions to make in drawing the ire and fire of armed forces leaders. This blunder came back after the war to haunt union membership when military people belittled the contributions of Merchant Seamen during the war and actively lobbied against benefits for them. Long skilled at maneuvering in political waters, the Navy managed to exert de facto authority over the merchant service all during the war. The Navy also gained by the U.S. Coast Guard becoming responsible for the inspection of merchant ships' seaworthiness and for the examination, licensing and certification of Merchant Marine personnel.

Stormy political waters swirled around the Merchant Marine during and after WW II. At Midway in 1942, there was a report that each member of the crew of the SS Nira Luckenbach had received $1,000 and refused to unload war materials on Sunday unless they were paid overtime. The truth was that there were no facilities and manpower capable of unloading the hazardous cargo of bombs and barrels of gasoline at Midway atoll.

The ship's captain proceeded to unload as best he could with his small crew. No Merchant Marine crew ever refused to unload their ship during WW II.

Another tall tale originated from Kuluk Harbor, Alaska, and involved the SS Thomas Jefferson, a Liberty ship. Reportedly, a U.S. destroyer approached a docked merchant ship and asked for a line to be thrown to them. Allegedly, no one responded. They had already done their eight hours of work and had gone ashore. This story proved to be false as well. The trouble stemmed from the animosity between the master and an officer on the Navy destroyer after the master demanded a receipt for the fuel oil the destroyer had received.

Despite the published famous quotes of admiration of the Merchant Marine by our top leaders, Presidents Roosevelt and Truman; Generals Eisenhower, Marshall, MacArthur and Vandergrift; Admirals King, Land and Nimitz, our casualties of one in every 26, the highest of any service, including the Marine Corps, the Merchant Mariners to this day are deemed draft dodgers, drunks, not veterans, free loader seekers and many, many more derogatory and detractive descriptions. These are lies, lies and damn lies, and the Merchant Mariners are victims of all.

The Army, Navy and Marine Corps fought and won their many battles and had heavy casualties in WW II. However, it was well known by our top commanding admirals and generals that without the war materials delivered to their fighting men at the right time by the Merchant Mariners, WW II would almost certainly have been lost to the Axis powers. Europe was facing starvation when President Roosevelt sent our Liberty ships across the Atlantic under his "Lend Lease" program.

Britain's Unsung Yank Heroes

With WW II now many years behind us, the number of British citizens who can remember Vera Lynn singing "There'll Always Be an England" dwindles with each passing day. Equally fading from British thoughts are memories of one group of Americans who arguably did more than any other to keep Britain alive, particularly during those dark early days of the war.

Fading British memories aside, sadly enough, these valiant Americans have, for the same 66 years, been denied adequate recognition and compensation by their own government . . . a U.S. government that has largely dismissed their unique bravery and sacrifice.

Indeed, it was the U.S. Merchant Marine that largely made allied victory attainable. It took some 15 tons of supplies to support one soldier for one year, many of these supplies coming from the United States under a "Lend Lease" agreement and delivered by American mariners starting well before Pearl Harbor and America's entry into the War. Many of the foodstuffs and other supplies upon which the British civilian populace relied were also delivered by the U.S. merchant mariners.

These mariners lost 243 killed and 604 became POWs prior to Pearl Harbor, after which America immediately entered the War, and the ranks of American merchant seamen swelled from 55,000 to 250,000. Volunteers ranged from 16 to 78 years of age, many below military entry physical standards, but patriotic volunteers nonetheless.

In combat from the very moment they left port, they were attacked by submarines, surface raiders, bombers, kamikaze suicide pilots and land-based artillery. Some 1,500 ships were sunk with one in nine mariners losing his ship. About 9,300 mariners were killed and 12,000 injured. In fact, the U.S. Merchant Marine suffered the highest WW II rate of all American military services, with one in 26 killed, more than the U.S. Marines, about 1.5 times the death rate of the U.S. Army and more than 4.3 times that of the U.S. Navy.

Last to return home from the War, American mariners remained in war zones long after the fighting troops came home. Casualties continued as 54 ships struck mines after V-E and V-J Day.

When the American "GI Bill of Rights" was enacted in 1944, these mariners were denied benefits granted to all other military service personnel . . . even those who had spent the war at home behind desks. Such benefits included unemployment compensation, education, home or small business loans, priority status for postwar jobs, and medical care for disabilities. On the other hand, Britain, Canada, Norway and The Netherlands all provided compensatory benefits to their WW II mariners.

Finally, in 1987, three torpedoed mariners successfully sued the American government, resulting in limited veteran status for former mariners in January 1988, far too late.

H. D. "Hap" Bledsoe - Experience at the End of World War II

I graduated from high school in June of 1942 and began at San Diego State College that fall, as the war in both the Pacific and Europe heightened. It became obvious to me that I should enter into military service. When I signed to join the U.S. Maritime, I was led to believe it was a full-fledged service like the Army, Navy or Marine Corps. In December of 1942, I was sent to boot camp in Catalina, CA, for training much like the Navy's indoctrination with uniforms and all. In March of 1943, with a Coast Guard Fireman Water Tender's License and a U.S. Maritime rating and passport, I was placed aboard a cargo ship for the invasion of Attu. I was 19 years of age.

Over the next few years, I was assigned to a number of ships and sailed all through the South Pacific until I had accumulated enough sea time to apply for officer's school. Again, in full uniform and dress

formality, I began a four-month cram engineering session to prepare me to go before the Coast Guard to sit for a Marine Steam and Diesel License to operate Merchant ships of unlimited horse power. At that time, I was issued a Lieutenant's commission by the U. S. Maritime Service; and the Navy, because they needed the Merchant Marines, issued me a Lieutenant's commission in the Navy Reserves.

For the rest of the war, I sailed on numerous vessels throughout the South Pacific and ended with a trip to Hong Kong, Singapore, Bombay, the Mediterranean Sea and finally New York where the ship was turned over to the Navy. I was retired and left on my own to get back home to San Diego any way I could.

Five months after returning to San Diego, I was diagnosed with tuberculosis which I had picked up in the Lingayen Gulf (north of Manila) where we spent four weeks aboard a ship. We then worked for four months straight without a day off - 4 hours on and eight hours off.

With all of my credentials and licenses, the doctors treating me, who did chest surgery at the San Diego Navy Hospital, tried to get me into the Navy hospital. The Navy hospital rejected me, claiming that I was a civilian. We next turned to the California State Hospital where I was rejected because they claimed I was military. Finally, the Health Department that had to get me off the streets because of the tuberculosis, put me in quarantine in the San Diego County Tuberculosis Center for four months. When I was released, I was told not to work for six months, as I had a cavity in my lung and the doctors didn't know if the streptomycin they gave me would retard the tuberculosis or if it would return.

With no place to live and no rehabilitation pay like veterans from the other services received, I was forced to move home with my mother *and stepfather. When I was rejected as a military member, I applied for California unemployment but was rejected claiming I was military and paid by the government. Two months later I received a call from the Unemployment Department stating that the U.S. Government had passed a bill to pay the rehabilitation to U.S. Merchant Marine members. However, after signing up for this benefit, six weeks in a row passed without receiving a check. I was informed that U. S. Government had agreed to pay for rehabilitation but did not appropriate any money for it. Finally, low and behold, one year and four months later, I received six $20.00 checks. It's a good thing I had a mother and friends and am a light eater or I would have starved waiting for our country to recognize those who served.*

Fortunately, even without a college education, I was able to succeed in business. I carry my own medical insurance and have not to this day used a military hospital or military benefits. Unfortunately, many members of the Merchant Marines were killed or wounded, neglected and forgotten by the very country we love and served.

The Myth

There is the myth --used as a justification for not granting a "Bill of Right" package to merchant seamen -- that they were overpaid, self-centered mercenaries working for high wages. They were an organized union force of war profiteers. None of that is true. The shipping companies and the allied cause received excellent value for what they paid. Admittedly, there were heavy drinkers in the ranks of the Merchant Marine. At sea our conduct becomes casual. We have a job to do and a ship to sail. Officers are not addressed as "sir" and we do not wear uniforms showing our rank and medals. We operate with a skeleton crew. The U.S. Navy needed 220 men to operate a Liberty ship "attack transport." Merchant Marine Liberty ships ran with only 45. In general the Navy has two men or three stationed where mariners have one.

When we are at a training camp, campus or military function, we wear uniforms and salute. As to drinking, we were not supposed to drink on board and certainly not on watch. My answer to the reason I drank during the war was that with our tanker sailing tomorrow, a torpedo may hit that engine room and I'll be dead. So I will have a good time ashore tonight.

A young ordinary seaman on the SS Gateway City, in the ill-fated Convoy PQ-17 making the Murmansk Run, received $3,000 for 13 months of the war's most dangerous work. This included an unpaid period of 172 days with ships laid up in Iceland while German scout planes watched them and the actual running of the gauntlet to Murmansk through the most dangerous waters in the world. His earnings amounted to just $231 a month.

Comparing a U.S. Navy Chief Petty Officer to a Merchant Marine able-bodied seaman, both with a wife and two children and 20 years at sea, the Chief Petty Officer earned $385.50 per month including

$251.10 basic pay plus $37.50 hazardous duty and $96.90 for his dependents. The able-bodied seaman earned $405 per month including $110 basic pay plus $110 war bonus and $60 (approximate) overtime and $125 if bombed. A point always overlooked is that members of the armed forces pay no federal or state income taxes, and U.S. Navy personnel receive a long list of hidden benefits that saves them substantial amounts of money.

When merchant seamen left their ships, even if their ship was torpedoed, their pay was terminated. They had to pay all of their expenses and had no workman's compensation or unemployment insurance. This was also the case if their ship was sunk and they became POWs. When the U.S. Navy attempted to take over the Merchant Marine in the early 1940, the head of the National Maritime Union that represented seamen on the East Coast, Joe Curran, fought back. In a union publication one reason for the Navy's effort was that the union had exposed various government agencies with respect to safety equipment, inadequate arming, improper stowage of cargo, etc. Mr. Curran was also referring to the early months of the war when many American merchants were torpedoed off the east coast and the Caribbean, killing more than a thousand civilian seamen. Those ships were mostly unarmed and effective systems had not yet been instituted. Seventeen minutes before the attack on Pearl Harbor a Jap sub torpedoed and sank the SS Cynthia Olsen.

Our merchant service was blasted by the press, particularly by Hearst newspaper columnists Walter Winchell and Westbrook. Winchell's attacks reached 50 million Americans in his broadcasts to "Mr. and Mrs. America and all the ships at sea." He accused the National Maritime Union merchant seamen on the east coast of being communist sympathizers who were putting mercury and emery dust into the engines and were overpaid. The union sued Winchell for $1 million but received only a few thousand. His claims were totally unfounded and were in the tradition of the "yellow journalism" and hysteria we saw in the 2012 presidential campaign. The

Hearst press machine inflamed the minds of American citizens and their military and political leaders. This is ongoing in the U.S. Congress to this day-since WW II ended. We were regarded for a few moments as heroes whose efforts probably saved our country.

Walter Winchell probably kept up his ultra-critical commentary going until his death at age 77 in 1972. During the "Cold War" of the 1950-60s, one of our engineers was sitting outside his room resting in the darkness after a tough day of business with the Russians. He was looking out at Europe's longest river, the Volga, when he heard the high-pitched sound of an aircraft engine coming up the river. A strange appearing boat came by at a very high speed on the water in the darkness. When our engineer returned to the States and described what he had seen, it became a high interest subject in several agencies. What are the Russians up to in secrecy? The final policy from Washington was to make no big secret costly action to design, build, operate and test out a Hydrofoil by MARAD, GE and Grumman Aircraft. The project took more than three years to complete. I worked on this project along with two other Merchant Marine engineers and a 2nd officer. We were graduates of the USMMA. The captain was a USNA grad.

We sailed the HS Denison from NY to Miami, FL and Portland, ME demonstrating the vessel at ports along the way to determine if there was any commercial interest. Our design called for a top speed of 60 knots (69 mph). That speed was easily reached, but she would go out of automatic and manual control at 62 or 63 knots speed. Late one afternoon after a full day of testing and logging, we were ordered to the Merchant Marine Pier at the Academy for a news media showing. That NYC cadre of news hounds, male and female, bore down on us with every question they could think of. Of course, they had no concept at all of a power boat or ship. Among that group was an aging Walter Winchell who watched us maneuver out. He was said to have looked out in the bay and commented for publication: "If those idiot engineers and technicians get the speed up to 60 knots on that tub, it will explode and kill every one of them."

WW II era unions also wanted to maintain their own power base which would erode if their membership fell under military control. In alliance with the unions, the shipping company owners wanted to keep their lucrative contracts. The U.S. Navy honestly felt that military control of civilian seamen and ships allowed the Allies to be more efficient.

Early in the war, another important element contributed to the high number of deaths on the East Coast and the Caribbean. U-boats at night were easily able to see the ships profiled against the lights of American coastal cities and torpedo them. Too many cities such as Miami, Atlantic City and Jacksonville refused to impose blackouts at night until forced to do so. The day after the SS Gulf America was torpedoed by the German U-boat 123 on April 10, 1942, killing 17 crew members and two Navy armed guards off Jacksonville Beach, Governor Spessard Holland ordered a blackout of all lights along Florida's longest coast of all the states that could be seen at sea and would silhouette passing ships.

Service Canteens & Rail Travel Discounts

During WW II, canteens for those in the service for their country were set up in our larger cities where a tired, hungry member of the armed services could rest and be served a soft drink and a sizeable snack while waiting for his ordered transportation. Rail transportation from NYC by at least one or more lines allowed sizeable discounts to servicemen.

Merchant Mariners could not partake of these hospitalities because they were not in uniform. As a Cadet/Midshipman of the U. S. Merchant Marine Academy and a sworn-in U.S. Naval Reserve, we wore our uniforms when in our home country.

In an NYC canteen my uniform was recognized as my being from the nearby USMMA and was told that I could not be served or rest there.

At the NYC RR station, I was also identified and told I had to pay full price for my ticket to my home in Virginia. There were several service-men nearby. I walked over where the clerk couldn't see me and introduced myself to the first soldier I saw. He said, "I know who you are and what you guys have done in this war." I asked him to please take my money and buy a ticket for me to Virginia. He said, *"I'll be glad to." He came back with my ticket and change.*

After the war ended we had to make trips from the British refinery at Abadan, Iran to the Island City of Singapore with our T-2 tanker to supply them with fuel. It was a busy bunkering port and amazing how quickly that city returned to its former prewar status and economy.

The Raffles Hotel, the playground/vacation site of every known and really wealthy celebrity male and female on the planet, was back in business. My roommate C/M John and I decided to see if we might have our lunch at this famous place built by Sir Stamford Raffles in the 1800's. We put on our best uniforms and shined our shoes as if preparing for regimental inspection. At the important buildings they had huge seven foot one or two Hindu Sikhs as doormen.

John and I strode up to the entrance in military steps and were politely ushered into the huge restaurant. We chose a table where we could look out of the huge open door. The food was absolutely delicious in comparison to the officers' mess on our ship.

About the time we were having our dessert there was a loud conversation outside. We peered out and saw that two gentlemen were being denied entrance because they were not wearing suitable clothes for entry to the

Raffles. They were our Chief Mate and Chief Engineer who saw their Cadets being treated as officers having their lunch.

John and I dared not tell anyone on the SS San Pasqual about that situation. Those two Sr. Officers would have been the laughingstocks by every man on that ship. We never told our Captain about this because he just might have found it humorous. John and I would have more work and study to do had that simple word gotten out from us.

Tales from the Author

Admiral Ernest J. King and Our Assignment to the British

Admiral Ernest J. King was highly intelligent and extremely capable but controversial. Some considered him as one of the greatest Admirals of the 20th century. We American Merchant Mariners and others point out that his "Anglophobia" (hate or fear of England or anything English) led him to make decisions which cost us 1,500 to 2,000 lives or more in 1942 and 1943 and beyond on the eastern seaboard and in the Caribbean. Convoys and blackouts were British proposals. He also refused, until March 1942, the loan of British convoy escorts when the USN had only a handful of suitable vessels. Instead of convoys, Admiral King had the U.S. Navy and Coast Guard perform scheduled antisubmarine patrols. German U-boat commanders learned the schedules and coordinated their attacks. Two million tons of cargo were lost in January and February 1942, alone. King was much disliked by his subordinate officers and enlisted men. But he was aggressive in driving his destroyer captains to attack U-boats in defense of convoys and in planning counter measures against German surface raiders.

Our new T-2 tanker, the SS San Pasqual, a U.S. "WET ink" (War Emergency Tanker Inc.) flying the Stars & Stripes, and a crew of Americans in early 1945 was assigned to the British as an auxiliary tanker vessel. We had never heard the word "Anglophobia" and wouldn't know what it meant anyway. However, we soon had enough of those five day shuttle runs in the Persian Gulf to the huge refineries in Abadan, Iran and back to Aden, Yemen. We were glad to get to Australia and a few other places in the Empire for a change now and then. Once we were sent to a tiny American post off the coast of Borneo. Cold American beer and American movies were great. Those Brits drink their sorry tasting beer at room temperature.

Michael James Monahan

There is a lonely grave in San Lorenzo Cemetery at St. Augustine, FL. No one knew who the man was that was buried there. We know little about him except he gave his life for his country. In April 1942, a body washed up on St. Augustine Beach. Papers found on him identified the body as Afro-American *Michael James Monahan*. The coroner listed his death as due to exposure in the Atlantic after being torpedoed. Fifty-three years later a reporter for the St. Augustine Record, digging through old files, found a short article about a man's body being washed ashore at St. Augustine Beach. Reporter Mike Grogan found where the grave was located with the help of the cemetery personnel and finding the death certificate, but there was no stone. A member of the AMMV, St. Johns River Chapter, saw the story and sent it to John Lockhart, a WW II Mariner vet, who was then the Editor of the St. Johns River Light. He found that Michael James Monahan had been a machinist on the SS Gulf America when it was torpedoed and shelled off Jacksonville Beach on April 10, 1942. He was from Covington, KY and had no known family. A marker was placed on his grave.

Seaman Monahan is one of the very few who lost his life at sea but is buried on land and is not forgotten. The U.S. Maritime Commission and War Shipping Administration named a Liberty ship for him that was built at the J. A. Jones Company's yard at Panama City, FL. The name of the ship is the SS Michael James Monahan. The late Mariner Henry Billitz used to take flowers to his wife's grave in the cemetery and would stop by Mr. Monahan's grave and leave a few of his flowers there.

There is something to be said about the deterioration of the American Merchant Marine between wars such as there was between WW II and WW I. The crew members of those old "rust buckets" were poorly paid and treated by the shipping company employers, and their only salvation was to join unions and negotiate a contract. New ships were being built by the War Shipping Administration, and a few of those old sailors joined the new ships as crew members. They all seemed to be story tellers of the old miserable past they called "the blue linen days" when that cheapest cloth was the sheets and covers for their bunks. Often they were paid in useless "Script" or nothing at all. With urging by the seaman's unions, Congress passed a law that required payment in U. S. cash at the end of a voyage.

Smokey Joe

Old "Smokey Joe", a fireman water tender on our new T-2 tanker, the SS San Pasqual, was from that earlier period before the war with his tales about going out to sea. Poor Joe had a bad speech impediment, but he was really a nice old man who tried to do his job well. Every time he went on watch in the fire room, smoke billowed from the stack. That was a no-no lest a U-boat sees it, and it showed the forced air and the fuel were not in balance. Joe dreaded maneuvering into port. He finally asked me as the engine cadet if I could come down and help him. Of course, I had to know about maneuvering. The first bell from the bridge as usual was to slow the engine, and the boilers' water level went high. The Chief Engineer came storming in yelling, "Joe, you've filled those SOBs already. When are you going to learn?" Then he saw me opening the return valve for control and departed. Joe said, "Cadet, that f----g chief gives me hell all the time and never teaches me anything." The Chief Engineer never came back again to check the boiler room and left me to teach Joe how to control the two boilers and their feed pump when maneuvering into a fuel dock.

We went to an Australian military camp on an island in the Indian Ocean who needed some few dozen barrels of fuel for their generator. Our captain was not happy to take a huge tanker into such a place and take a few days to fill their barrels. The smallest cargo pump we had was a stream reciprocating stripping pump that was used to clean the cargo tanks when we had to clean them. We spilled a lot of fuel because we could not get that pump to run slow enough. There was just nothing there except what the Aussies had brought in. One day we were walking near the camp when some four or five wild natives with spears and knives, carrying some three packages, came up to see the officer in charge of the camp. It was obvious that he took their packages and gave them money.

We two cadets used our lowest officer rank to ask the Australian camp commander what we were seeing in his transaction with those primitive warriors. The war was over but there were many Japanese soldiers hiding out in the territories they had controlled. The Australian commander said that he was buying Japanese heads, and he had to pay a good price to avoid the Japs coming up with enough money to buy his head.

That area had seen a lot of combat, and there was a small bridge that had been damaged in the fighting. Joe and the other fireman water tender called Junior were walking about until it became a little dark. They took a short way back to the ship because one or both had to go on watch. The stairs on one end of the bridge across the small stream had been completely blown away. Both of them fell to the ground, and Joe couldn't get up. He had no control from his waist down. Junior got the Aussies to carry him to their camp where they said they could get him to one of their hospitals and then send him to a U.S. hospital who would send him home to the U.S. The Chief Engineer went to see Joe and talked to the Australians about taking proper care of him. When the Chief returned to the ship, I asked him about Joe's condition and what he thought about it. He just smiled and said, "Smokey Joe's going to be all right. He's telling those exaggerated lie stories like he always did. He told me he fell off that bridge so hard the Aussies had to dig him out with picks and shovels.

Port Moresby

This is the capital of the large island of New Guinea where we once answered a call for fuel. Fighting had gone on there with the Japanese from February 2, 1942 until April 12, 1943. The U. S. Army finally trained a picked command of their tough mountaineers that defeated the Japs for good. They drove them off through the rugged, huge wood area and off over the mountains on the north side of the Island. The town was destroyed and deserted, and they had only makeshift small fuel handling capability.

Thus this area was a strategic target for the Japanese invasion to conduct a direct sea/land amphibious assault in May 1942, but the invasion was prevented in the historic Battle of Coral Sea, the first of five carriers versus sea battles in mankind's history. As was long anticipated by General MacArthur, the Japanese kept trying to reach Port Moresby. Their strategic bid for air dominance by setting up a network of bases commanding the sea lines was obvious, as was their desire to isolate and cut off Australia as a war aim. But MacArthur, with a mixed command, was reorganizing and training upon the fly. Many Australian units were drilling with wooden mockups of rifles in August 1942 before MacArthur's people could get set up in his planned defensive bases set up on the north coast. Finally war materials began to trickle in from the States in July.

As the Supreme commander of the South Pacific area, General Douglas MacArthur had, after months of arguments with that victory, convinced the Australian politicians in early August of 1942 to *defend Australia by defending Port Moresby.*

We were still operating our U.S. Wartime Emergency Inc. T-2 tanker as a British Wartime Auxiliary vessel. As expected, the Captain and the Chief Mate were not pleased in having to move a huge tanker into small, makeshift fuel discharge facilities.

More on the Japanese

Wholesale surrenders of a thousand of British and Australian troops at Singapore and the American and Filipino defeats at Bataan and Corregidor seemed to convince the Japanese of the utter weakness of the Allies armed forces and their inferiority to the Japanese military.

The Japanese POWs saw capture as a personal disgrace to family and country. They planned acts of rebellion, refused to work or take orders from anyone but their superior officers, and considered suicide an ever-present alternative. Dying was their only honorable answer. No letters were sent or received. Japanese POWs will not worship in shrines erected for them in camps. It's sacrilege to enter a shrine built on enemy territory.

It would appear that the Japanese military figure adhered to the ultimate degree to what their field service manual called Senjinkun. The Japanese soldier was not permitted to be a prisoner of war, and the ultimate disgrace was to surrender. Since dying was the only honorable answer, this was the underlying reason for the Japanese treatment toward their prisoners of war in WW II.

Japanese wartime, outlandish, terrible treatment of the POWs and civilian captives still remains in the minds of the leaders and people in the Far East to this day. China and South Korea must face up to its history. "It was a breach of women's rights committed during wartime as well as a violation of universal human rights" according to a translation of a recent speech by South Korea President Lee Myung-bak. The sexual enslavement of Korean girls and women is called by several names; we Americans refer to those unfortunate females in English as *"Pleasure Girls"* and tend to forget it.

But Lt. Stanley Willner, who spent three and a half years as a Japanese POW and worked on the bridge over the River Kwai, didn't forget. When he and his friend, Lt. Dennis Roland, attended *The March of Forgiveness* eight years later said, *"I can't Forget or Forgive"* and refused to walk across the bridge with him, and watched from afar.

On March 1, 1945, the SS Columbia was approaching one of the western beaches of the island of Iwo Jima to deliver ammunition to the Marine Corps headquarters there. As the vessel neared the shore, two Japanese batteries opened fire, wounding a man on the aft deck-fan tail. Thousands of U. S. Marines were at that base and could have been killed in a huge explosion of that ammo carrier. Thinking quickly, the ship's captain changed course and moved out of range with his new Victory class turbine engine. He wondered if he had a slower Liberty ship could he have made it out of there. Some Victory ships were named after black Merchant Mariners killed and important black Americans who worked in the shipyards.

Some brave enterprising crews of merchant ships rigged up telephone poles and wire to look like guns fore and aft. Second Mate Allen H. Knox told the story years later that they used 8x8 timbers with covers over them. The vessel was the MS Cape Henry, a brand new C-1 class cargo ship. It sailed into the Gulf of Mexico with its holds full of ammunition. The U.S. massive ship building got underway in 1936 in light of the probability of a second WW in Europe.

The U.S. Merchant Marine, while not a military service, fought a war on many fronts. Private companies that owned and operated merchant ships' auxiliary naval vessels had enemies at home and in every ocean.

The End of the War

Port Moresby on the large island of New Guinea was one of our ports of call for fuel. There were three tall destroyed tanks and one new uncompleted tank in the completely abandoned city which I believe was a Dutch colony before the war. An Aussie soldier was guarding a Japanese POW working on the road who asked his guard if he could speak with us two Americans, and we agreed to speak with him. We were startled by his perfect speech in English. He said he was a professor of English language in the University at Tokyo and was drafted into the army as a sergeant. All he wanted to do, he said, was to get back to teaching at the University. There was a large cannon there that was intact but blown 20 feet from its mount. We were told it got the first American gun boat coming in, but it was instantly blown away and all its crew was killed when General MacArthur ordered the Navy to fire.

A very disturbing cruelty by the invading Japanese soldiers to the females living there, we were told, was the killing by knives and bayonets to their vaginal areas if they refused to submit to having sex with the Japs. At that time we knew the U.S., with the Germans and their allies out of WW II, were concentrating their forces for an invasion of the home islands of the Empire of Japan. We were advised to expect a million and more casualties to defeat the Japs at home. No one on our ship spoke of what we would be ordered to do, but they knew our runs from the British refinery to Abadan, Iran would be changed to General MacArthur's forces near the fighting on the beaches of Japan.

On August 6, 1945, our chief radio officer told us that a deadly atomic bomb had been dropped on a major Japanese city. "What the hell is an atomic bomb?" After three days with nothing from the Japanese on the 140,000 casualties at Hiroshima, another 70,000 were killed at Nagasaki and Emperor Hirohito declared the war over.

Our younger generations know little to nothing about the Japanese dreadful treatment and thousands of deaths they imposed on their POWs and citizens of the countries they overran by beatings, overwork, no medical attention, starvation, killings and native women and children held in POW camps. President Harry Truman ordered the atomic bombs dropped on those two heavily populated cities. These younger folks, such as the President's grandson, research a bit and are humanely shocked at the number of deaths and the greatest of destructions and feel very sorry for their families.

We few WW II Merchant Mariners still living in our 80s and 90s recall the atrocities and brutality toward POWs by the Japanese at every prison site and tend to view the Hiroshima and Nagasaki bombings as a disaster they brought on themselves.

During the war, my cousin, George, an expert naval machinist, disappeared. A secret phone number was given to his wife with orders not to call her husband unless there was an absolute family necessity. All he knew was that he was to make a big trigger mechanism from his and others ideas until it met a standard qualification and would definitely work. When the atomic bomb fell on Hiroshima, George and his fellow workers were astounded. They had developed *the trigger for the first atomic bomb* without knowing what they were doing beyond working on a very important project for the war effort in secrecy at Oak Ridge, Tennessee.

German Air Raid on Bari

In 1943, during the Italian Campaign, the port of Bari in southern Italy served as an important logistic hub for the Allied forces. Crucial ammunition, supplies and provisions were unloaded from ships at the ports, then transported to the Allied force attempting to capture Rome and push German forces out of the Italian peninsula to the north. Bari had inadequate air defenses, no RAF fighter squadrons.

Bari was a city of some 200,000 people with an old section dating back to the Middle Ages. New Bari had broad boulevards and modern buildings, built by Italian dictator, Benito Mussolini as an award for producing the most babies in a specified time period. Bari, old and new, had suffered little damage because the Allies earmarked the city as a major supply port from the start. On the afternoon of December 2, 1943, a German Messerschmitt Me-210 made a reconnaissance flight over the port of Bari, cruising at 23,000 feet and made a telltale contrail across the sky. The anti-aircraft crews on the ground showed little notice. The port was under the jurisdiction of the British due to Bari being the main supply base for General Montgomery's Eighth Army. As 1943 drew to a close, there was an influx of Allied shipping into the harbor. On December 2nd there were at least 30 Allied ships crowded into the harbor, packed so tightly they almost touched.

U.S. Fifteenth Air Force commander Maj. Gen. Jimmy Doolittle had arrived in Bari. The Americans had championed daylight precision bombing, but the Eighth Air Force in England was suffering terrible casualties in order to prove the theory. In addition to usual war material, Merchant ships moored in Bari carried aviation fuel for Doolittle's Air Force. Totally absorbed by the task of getting the Fifteenth Air Force on the ground, the Allies gave little thought to the possibility of a German air raid on Bari. The Allies thought the *Luftwaffe* was relatively weak in Italy and stretched so thin to mount a major effort. German reconnaissance flights over Bari were seen as a nuisance. British anti-aircraft batteries said, "Why waste the ammunition?" About 200 officers, 52 civilian technicians and several hundred enlisted men of the US Air Force were being brought into the city.

In the harbor merchant cargo ships and tankers waited their turn to be unloaded. Captain Otto of the Liberty Ship SS John Bascom went ashore to see if the process could be speeded up. There was some possibility in 1943 that the Germans just might use poison gas. By that time the Germans were on the defense on all fronts. They had sustained a major defeat in Russia at Stalingrad and had lost North Africa as well. The Allies were then in Europe inching up the Italian peninsula. It was said that Adolf Hitler was not a great advocate of chemical warfare because he had been gassed during WW I.

President Roosevelt issued a policy statement condemning the use of gas on any civilized nation, but he pledged that the US would reply in kind if an enemy used such weapons first. The merchant ship SS John Harvey was selected to convey a shipment of poison gas to Italy to be held in reserve should such a situation occur. The mustard gas bombs were loaded aboard the Liberty ship SS John Harvey and appeared to be conventional. They were 8 inches in diameter and 4 feet long and contained 60 to 70 pounds of gas. The poison gas shipment was shrouded in official secrecy. No single individual involved knew everything about it. Lt. Tom Richardson, the ship's cargo security officer, was the only one who officially knew about the mustard gas. His cargo manifest clearly listed 2,000 M47 A1 mustard gas bombs in the hold, about 100 tons. Richardson wanted to unload the SS John Harvey as soon as possible.

The Germans arrived on schedule at 7:30 p.m., but could hardly believe their eyes. The docks were brilliantly lit. Cranes stood out in sharp relief as they unloaded cargo from the ships gaping holds. The first bombs hit the city proper, but soon it was the harbor's turn.

Some 30 vessels were riding at anchor that night and each ship's crew had to respond as best they could. A good number of crew members were on shore leave with some crews shorthanded. German flares gave sailors the first inkling of the attack. Aboard the SS John Bascom, the second officer, Bill Rudolf, saw the flashes and alerted Captain Heitmann. Their gun crew sprang into action, joining the barrage of the shore batteries that were hurling into the sky. Tracer bullets laced the air, but the anti-aircraft was largely ineffective,

There was no time to cut anchor cables and get underway. Crews along the east jetty watched helplessly while a creeping barrage of German bombs became ever closer to their vulnerable vessels. The SS Joseph Wheller took a direct hit and exploded into flames; the SS John Motley was hit in its #five hold; the SS John Bascom anchored next to the John Motley was in line for punishment. The SS John Bascom shuddered under a rain of bombs from stem to stern. Captain Heitmann was lifted off his feet and slammed against the wheelhouse's door. Heitmann saw the body of Nicholas Elgin sprawled nearby from a head wound, his clothes torn off.

The entire harbor was hell on earth. Heitmann , ignoring his own wounds, ordered his crew into the single undamaged lifeboat. Yellow-orange flames leaped into the air, producing acrid smoke. Water surfaces were covered by a viscous scum of oil and fuel, blinding and choking those unfortunate enough to be in the water. Ships were in various stages of burning and sinking. When the flames reached munitions-laden holds, some exploded. Debris was everywhere.

Meanwhile, the crew of the SS John Harvey was engaged in a heroic effort to save their ship. It was still intact and had sustained no direct bomb damage. Nevertheless, she had caught fire and the situation was doubly dangerous with those mustard gas bombs. Captain Knowles, Lt. Beckstrom and others refused to leave their posts, but their heroism was ultimately in vain. Without warning the SS John Harvey blew up, disappearing in a huge mushroom-shaped fireball that hurled pieces of the ship and her cargo hundreds of feet into the air. Everyone on board was killed instantly.

Heitmann and his surviving crew managed to reach the tip of the east jetty around a lighthouse that was located at the north end. He had about 50 merchant mariners. Many were badly wounded and some were so badly burned that the slighted touch brought agony. At first the lighthouse seemed to be a refuge, but was soon deemed a deathtrap. A sea of flames cut off Heitmann and his men from following the jetty's long spine into the city where they might have been relatively safe and gotten some help.

While the sailors were waiting to be rescued, Ensign Vesole, commander of the SS John Bascom's armed guard detachment, was having difficulty breathing. Many other men were gasping but Vesole said, "I smell garlic" without realizing the implications of his remark. A garlic odor was a telltale sign of mustard gas. It had intermixed with the oil floating in the harbor and lurked with all the smoke in the area. A launch rescued Captain Heitmann and the other survivors from the east jetty, but their troubles were just beginning.

The American Merchant Marine sustained the highest losses, losing the Liberty ships John Bascom, John L. Motley. Joseph Wheller, Samuel J. Tilden, and John Harvey. Next morning survivors woke to a scene of devastation. There were more than 1,000 military and merchant marine casualties; about 800 were admitted to local hospitals. Fortunately, Bari was the site of several Allied military hospitals and related support facilities. Casualties from the raid began pouring in until the hospitals were filled to overflowing. Respiratory systems were badly irritated and the mustard gas casualties were wracking with coughs and had difficulty breathing and the doctors suspected some kind of chemical agent was involved.

Lt. Col. Alexander, an expert on chemical warfare medicine, was sent to Bari. He reported that it looked like mustard gas. British authorities finally admitted, off the record, they knew the merchant marine SS John Harvey was carrying poison gas. Alexander drew up a report detailing his findings that were approved by Gen. Eisenhower. Secrecy dogged the whole affair. Eventually the British and American people were told about the devastating Bari Raid, but they were never told about the mustard gas. There were

628 mustard gas casualties among Allied and the US Merchant Marine personnel. Of these 69 died within two weeks.

"Axis Sally," the infamous propaganda broadcaster, learned the truth and taunted the Allies. "I see you boys are getting gassed by your own poison gas" she sneered. As to "Axis Sally," our Radio Operators on watch could sometimes pick her up and advise us to come forward on the tanker to listen to her. She thought she was intimidating us with her speeches. But we viewed her as a source of entertainment because she always played American music to get attention. In 1948, Mildred Gillars, accused of being the wartime radio propagandist "Axis Sally," pleaded guilty in Washington, D.C. to charges of treason. She later was convicted and ended up serving 12 years in prison.

The attack, which had lasted a little more than one hour, put the port out of action until February 1944 and was called "Little Pearl Harbor." Bari is on the heel of the boot of Italy on the Adriatic Sea in Europe. Like Pearl Harbor, the military leadership never thought of a heavy aircraft attack and moored and tied up their ships too close to each other. And the attacking bomber forces obtained complete surprises and were able to bomb the harbors and their contents with great accuracy.

Winston Churchill, however, ordered that all British documents be purged, listing mustard gas deaths as "burns due to enemy actions." In 1986, the British government finally admitted to survivors of the Bari raid that they had been exposed to poison gas and their pension pay should be accordingly. U.S. records of the attack were declassified in 1959. That made no difference to the American Merchant Marines exposed to poison gas there, who had not at that date received a penny from their government. And as we now know in the closing days of 2012, those of us living in our mid 80's & 90's will expire without any compensatory benefit whatsoever in more than 47 years.

Storms and Hurricanes at Sea

Extremely foul weather at sea can be almost as dangerous and frightening as enemy attacks by armed ships and aircraft. Ships of all sizes and designs have been lost at sea with all hands. This has also happened in our Great Lakes well up into the past 20th century. Our Liberty ships had to contend with the weather as well as the enemies during the four years of WW II. The difference from the old salts that sailed the merchant vessels before the war was that these new crew members were all mostly quickly trained teenagers with young officers; and anyone who goes to sea for any period of time will experience discomfort, loss of sleep, sea sickness and vomiting again and again, or see it with his other members.

In heavy weather the propeller comes out of the water, shaking the whole stern of the ship, and she's rolling from side to side all the time. You stagger and fall into the bulkheads until you learn your "sea legs." The cooks have to use huge pots for cooking their meals. At the tables in the crew and officers' messes you have to be very careful when she rolls or you will have your meal in your lap or on the deck.

Liberty Ship Fighting Heavy Seas in the North Atlantic

Religion at Sea

In general, sailors are not considered religious. But there were plenty of prayers prayed under attack and facing death or a storm that could sink the vessel in two sections. The purser on the ship is the officer that reports to the captain and handles the money, the ship store, records and tasks for him that are not those of the stewards, deck or engine departments. Young Dean Beaumont was the purser on the Liberty ship SS Brander Matthews, and he was a very religious individual. Liberty ships were known to break in half during a storm, and the captain was concerned that could happen there. She was rolling up to 41 degrees at times. They were going to Mozambique to pick up a load of coal that allies needed in Italy.

A 16-year-old kid seaman was very frightened and went up to the bridge and into the wheelhouse where the officers were and asked, "Mr. Beaumont, are we sinking?" Dean stared at him and scanned all the damage to the ship he could see and replied, "I won't lie to you. There is a good chance we won't make it." The boy was deeply disturbed and said, "How can I be sure that I'll go to Heaven? I've never been to church so I don't know much, but some of those guys say you know all about it." Dean said, "It might be too late for you. We could sink any minute now." The boy said, "But there must be some way." Dean said, "All right, pray really hard to God, and if God believes you, He will try to help you." Tears ran down the boy's face as he tried to find some comfort. Dean put an arm around his shoulders.

There is no onboard entertainment, only books to read from the big trunk load of paperbacks brought aboard by the Navy Armed Guard. The crew had no movies or even comics. Sometimes a month old newspaper from the U.S. would show up in some various ports around the world which the young men found to their liking. The only musical instruments aboard were when some sailor would have brought a jew's-harp or harmonica from home because they would fit in his pocket. My father played both of these instruments in WW I and taught me to play them just before WW II started. After graduating from the US Merchant Marine Academy, and as third assistant engineer on a tanker going back and forth from our refinery in Mississippi to ports up north, it seemed all the music I heard was Cajun. So it took a few trips, but I learned to play Cajun songs well enough to play them with their makeshift bands "on the bayou."

WW II seamen had a lot of time on their hands after their work was through, but they never developed anything much but card games. They talked, listened to the radio programs from the Armed Forces Network and the Japanese propagandist, "Tokyo Rose," and ridiculed her. All seamen exchange sea stories any time two or more meet anywhere. It's an age-old tradition going back to the ancient times when vessels were rowed or sailed for moving on water. We WW II veterans are now all in our mid 80s and 90s and we still trade sea stories. Every ship is somewhat different even if built in the same shipyard. And every sailor has a different memory even if sailing on the same vessel. I just came across a statement that the Naval Armed Guards had the highest casualty list in the U.S. Navy, and it was higher than the Merchant Mariners. (Such lists were never published.

The Final Little Battle of Saipan

Out on the Pacific Ocean, the SS Brander Matthews sailed west with two other Liberty ships following a lightly-armed escort boat. Men stood on the decks of the vessels with binoculars, constantly on the alert for signs of the enemy. Captain Nielson mentioned the possibility of steering a zigzag course to create difficulties for submarines, but that would slow them down. Liberty ships were painfully slow, chugging along at 10 knots per hour or less if there were wind and seas running choppy. One morning the chief mate came to Dean Beaumont and said he had a deck hand that was seriously ill and was unable to perform his work. The pursers were all we had for doctors on merchant ships. The crewman said he had terrible pains in his stomach. Dean and the mate pretended the deck hand had appendicitis, and they were going to operate on him with some surgical equipment they said they had. The poor fellow immediately said he was feeling a lot better, got up from the bed, ran out of the room, and went quietly to work on deck.

When the small convoy reached their destination, the big battle of Saipan was over. But there were still Japanese raids in the area and reports of dead Japanese soldiers, sailors and pilots still on the grounds. The Japanese had lost the island and the military embarrassment was of such a magnitude that the notorious General Hideki Tojo was forced to resign on July 20, 1944 along with his entire cabinet. All three Liberty ships anchored out at the town of Garapan on the western shore of Saipan with the SS Brander Matthews close to the beach. The whole town had been leveled and there were no port facilities remaining. Army crews began unloading the steel boxes from the holds and bolting them together to form a long dock 24 feet wide and more than 100 feet long. The dock was set up so that the trucks could drive on top of it to unload other ships.

At 3:00 A.M., the General Quarters alarm sounded, and Dean intended to run for the door but forgot he was in the upper berth and tumbled on the steel deck and injured both knees. He had volunteered to be a loader and went running for the door but stubbed his foot on the one-inch coming of the threshold and went skidding across the steel deck on his face, creating an injury from hairline to the bottom of his jaw from which he still bears scars if he's still alive. Finally making it to the gun tub, he climbed in and loaded the antiaircraft gun for the Navy gunner who arrived seconds later. The ship still had its booms out since they were unloading during the day. The masts were attached to the booms with guy-wires about an inch and a half thick.

Three Japanese fighter planes swooped down at the ships, bullets flying from their machine guns. American shore batteries opened up and the sky grew bright with tracer fire. Dean saw one of the aircraft diving toward his ship, peppering the superstructure and decks with bullets. As the plane strafed the Liberty ship, Navy gunners on the side decks fired antiaircraft guns while men on the fore and aft decks fired three & 5 inch guns. Dean leaned over on one side of the gun tub and picked up an ammo box without noticing in all that commotion that a two-ton boom was falling straight toward him. A young Navy gunner on the other side of the ship had shot the main mast and the wires holding the boom. Dean straightened his body and stood up with a load of ammunition just as the boom slammed into the exact spot where he had been seconds before. The boom smashed in the side of the gun tub and bent over the edge of the ship.

Shore batteries and Armed Guard crews kept firing at the planes and finally the attackers soared away into the night. The young Navy gunner had missed the battle phone command from the Armed Guard Officer on the bridge who was telling the gunners on one side or the other port or starboard to open fire or hold fire. The ships were damaged, and a dozen men were injured. No one was killed or seriously injured.

"It was really close and the Lord was good to me," said Dean Beaumont. "God saved my life."

The gunnery mistake was a common occurrence with those Liberty ships. Many of those ships' machine guns did not have keepers to restrict their turning radius, and the gunners fired bullets across the deck and past the wheelhouse. The US Congress was always concerned by the costs of ships. Naval vessels are very careful with their guns' firing radiuses during construction and sea trials.

The Marines and Army were in charge of the island of Saipan and invited the Merchant Mariners to come ashore to watch the movies that were brought out in a big truck. Nothing was left of the town so they sat in the sand and enjoyed the movies.

JR Gunderson and Hank Rosen

"JR" was only 20 during WW II on the Merchant Liberty ship. During the Korean War, "JR" joined the Army and was an early member of the 101st Airborne Rangers Division. His daughter thanked Ian Allison and me for our wartime service to our country and our continuing to try to get recognition and benefits for our men. She said it makes her so sad that our government has done nothing, and will probably do nothing, despite our and others hard efforts. Junior "JR" B. Gunderson received a full Military Honor Guard for his funeral service and burial. Many military groups asked what they could do. Sandra said her Dad would have loved his services and was so pleased that in response to her letter before he passed on that I said we were considering publishing a book on us Merchant Marine veterans in WW II that will surely have "Old JR" Gunderson's name in it.

Excerpts from Statement of Herman "Hank" Rosen at H.R. 23 House Hearing, April 18, 2007
Mr. Rosen:

Thank you, Mr. Chairman. My name is Herman Rosen. I'm known as Hank. On April 29, 2007, I will be 88 years old. I live in San Diego.

I applied to the U.S. Merchant Marine Academy in March 1942 soon after the Japanese attacked Pearl Harbor. I was sworn in as a Cadet USMMA and Midshipman USNR, and reported to the Academy at Kings Point, NY. After three months of preliminary training, I shipped out from Wilmington, NC on the new SS John Drayton, a Liberty ship. We sailed to New York and loaded Douglas bombers, Sherman tanks, ammunition and supplies for the Russian troops who were battling the Germans at Stalingrad.

Due to the horrendous Merchant Marine losses of ships and men in the North Atlantic, the SS John Drayton was routed from New York to Cuba, through the Panama Canal, to the Pacific Ocean, down the west coast of South America and across the Atlantic to South Africa. In Durban, we joined a convoy that traveled through the

Indian Ocean to the Arabian Sea and finally to the Persian Gulf and Khorsamshar, Iran. It was a journey of 17,260 miles from October 1942 to February 1, 1943. Our cargo was finally unloaded on April 1, and we were ordered to return to the States.

On a dark night 21 days later, with gale force winds blowing, the SS John Drayton was trapped, torpedoed and sunk by two Italian submarines some 300 miles due east of Durban, South Africa. I scrambled to a lifeboat. I injured my leg and joined 23 other frightened, injured, oil-covered Merchant Mariners and Navy gun crew. As was the policy at that time, my pay as Merchant Mariner ceased the moment I jumped into the lifeboat. The Navy gun crew's pay continued. We spent 30 days and nights adrift in the Indian Ocean without food or potable water. We drank sea water, salt water, urine and blood. Nineteen men in that boat died; five survived.

We were finally picked up by a Greek vessel and taken to a military hospital in Durban. I weighed 97 pounds and suffered from exposure, malnutrition, dehydration, septic abrasions of hands and feet, conjunctivitis of both eyes, shock and tachycardia. After several months of hospitalization, during which time I was not paid, I returned to the Academy, graduated and was commissioned as Ensign U.S. Naval Reserve and licensed as Third Mate in the Merchant Marine. On graduation from Kings Point you have the choice of going into the Navy, Army, Marine Corps or Air Force. Education is great there. I continued sailing throughout the war and finally became Acting Chief Officer, and was discharged from the Merchant Marine at war's end. It is noteworthy that the Merchant Mariners in my lifeboat, in the boat, and the hospital were not paid a dime. The Navy gun crews were paid – same boats, same guys, same hospitals – they were paid, we were not.

In 1944, the GI Bill of Rights was passed, but the Merchant Mariners received no veteran's status or benefits. We received no 52 weeks of *pay at $20 per week. This does not sound like much these days, but in those days my parents paid $30 for an apartment. Bread was ten cents a loaf. Milk was ten cents a quart. $20 a week was substantial. We received no VA loans, no veteran's health benefits, no family tax relief, no VA burial, no generous life insurance or no mortgage interest deductions.*

We suffered the highest proportion of casualties of any branch of the armed services. More than 9,000 Merchant seamen died and more than 700 American ships were sunk. It has been a long hard battle for us to get veteran status. I ask you today to rectify that wrong. When I die, I will have a flag and can be buried in a military cemetery. I can go to a VA hospital, but I have to pay because I'm not penurious (extremely poor.)

Excerpts from Statement of William Jackson

My name is William A. Jackson. I'm 88 years old and have been working in the Merchant Marine since 1935. I shipped out at the early age of 16 as a busboy on a merchant ship, passenger ships and freighters. Before the U.S. entered the war, I volunteered to sail on ships loaded with ammunition, tanks and cargo headed for the Red Sea. We took it to the Canal Zone for British forces where we witnessed two air raids. Two Merchant ships were damaged and sunk.

On December 7, 1941, I was at home in San Francisco when Pearl Harbor was bombed. I decided I would contact my classmates at Oakland High School. We had an ROTC unit there, and I was the only African-American in that unit. Together we went down to the Army recruiting station, and there was a mixture of all races. I noticed they called all the other guys and assigned them. They sent me home. I asked why, and the lady said, "I'm sorry, but we don't have a place for African-American soldiers." I became very angry and told them, "Don't ever try to draft me. I just returned from the war zone already in the Merchant Marine. I'm going back to get a ship." On December 9, I was assigned to the SS Panama and continued to sail.

In August 1942, I was on a ship that was sunk in enemy action. I was hospitalized in Trinidad for four and a half months without pay, because when a Merchant ship went down your pay stopped. Everybody else was paid. I think people don't realize that. (Mr. Bill Jackson eventually made it up the ladder to Chief Engineer. It took quite a long time, but he was persistent.)

Port Chicago Disaster

The Port Chicago disaster was a deadly munitions explosion that occurred on July 17, 1944 at the Port Chicago Naval Magazine in Port Chicago, California. Munitions detonated while being loaded onto a Merchant Marine cargo vessel bound for the Pacific Theater of Operations, killing 320 sailors and civilians and injuring 390 others. Most of the dead and injured were enlisted African-American sailors. The town was located on Suisun Bay in the estuary of the Sacramento and San Joaquin Rivers. Suisun Bay is connected to the Pacific Ocean by San Francisco Bay. In 1944, the town was a little more than a mile from the Navy munitions depot. The magazine was planned in 1941 with construction beginning shortly after the attack on Pearl Harbor. The first ship to dock was loaded on December 8, 1942.

Munitions transported through the magazine included bombs, shells, naval mines, torpedoes and small arms ammunition. Munitions were delivered to Port Chicago by rail then individually by hand, crane and winch onto Merchant cargo ships for transport to the war combat zones. Since April 1944, when Captain Kinne assumed command of Port Chicago, the loading officers had been pushing the enlisted men to load the explosive cargoes very quickly. Ten short tons per hatch per hour had been set by his superior at the Mare Island Navy Yard. Kinne tallied each crew's average tonnage per hour. Junior officers placed bets with each other in support of their 100-man crews, called "divisions," and coaxed their crews to load more than the others.

Coast Guard Commander Paul B. Cronk, head of the Coast Guard explosive-loading detail task with supervision of the working dock, warned the Navy that conditions were unsafe and ripe for disaster. The Navy refused to change its procedures and Cronk withdrew the detail.

The Merchant Marine Liberty ship SS E. A. Bryan docked at the inboard, landward side of Port Chicago's 1,500 ft. pier at 8:15 a.m. on July 13, 1944. The ship arrived at the dock with empty cargo holds, but it was carrying 5,292 barrels of bunker C heavy fuel for its upcoming trip across the Pacific Ocean. At 10:00 a.m., seamen from the ordinance battalion began loading the ship with munitions. After four days of around the clock loading, 4,600 tons of explosives had been stored in its hold. The ship was about 40% full by the evening of July 17. (Bunker C fuel is sticky and black and is used to fire the boilers of steam ships. It is the waste oil left over from the refined products such as gasoline and kerosene. It is not highly combustible, but it burns hot with a lot of black smoke and is cheap.)

At 10:00 p.m. on July 17, Division Three's 98 men were loading SS E. A. Bryan with 1,000 bombs into No. 3 hold, 40mm shells into No. 5 hold and fragmentation cluster bombs into No. 4 hold. Incendiary bombs were being loaded as well; those bombs weighed 650 pounds each and were "live." They had their fuses installed. The incendiary bombs were being loaded carefully one at a time into No. 1 hold that might have a winch brake that might have been inoperative.

A box car delivery contained a new airborne antisubmarine depth charge design. The Mark 47 armed with 252 pounds of torpex was being loaded carefully one at a time into No. 1 hold. Torpex charges were more sensitive than TNT (dynamite) to external shock and container dents. On the pier, resting on three parallel rail spurs, were 16 rail cars holding about 430 tons of explosives. In all, the munitions in the ship contained the equivalent of about 2,000 tons of TNT. The 102 men of the Sixth Division were busy rigging the newly built Merchant Victory ship, the SS Quinault, in preparation for loading it with explosives beginning at midnight.

A total of 67 officers and the Merchant Mariners crew of the two ships were at their stations, and various support personnel were present such as the three-man civilian train crew and a Marine sentry. Nine Navy officers and 29 armed guards watched the procedure. A Coast Guard fire barge with a crew of five was docked at the pier. An officer who left the docks after 10:00 p.m. noticed that the men of Division Three were having trouble pulling munitions from rail cars because they had been packed so tightly.

At 10:18 p.m., witnesses reported hearing a noise described as a "metallic sound and rending timbers, such as made by a falling boom." Immediately afterward an explosion occurred on the pier and a fire started. Five to seven seconds later a more powerful explosion took place as the majority of the ordnance within and near the Merchant ship SS E. A. Bryan detonated in a huge fireball some three miles in diameter. Chunks of glowing, hot metal and burning ordnance were flung more than 12,000 feet into the air. The E. A. Bryan was completely destroyed and the Quinault was blown out of the water, torn into sections and thrown in every direction. The stern section landed upside down in the water 500 feet away. The Coast Guard fire boat CG-60014-F was thrown 600 feet upriver where it sank.

The pier, along with the box cars, locomotive, rails, cargo and men, was blasted to pieces. Nearby boxcars waiting within their revetments to be unloaded at midnight were bent inward and crumpled by the force of the shock. The port's barracks and other buildings and much of the surrounding town were severely damaged. Shattering glass and a rain of jagged metal and undetonated munitions caused many additional injuries between both military and civilian populations, although no one outside the immediate pier area was killed. Nearly $9.9 million worth of damage was caused to U. S. Government property. Seismographs at the University of California, Berkeley, sensed the two shock waves traveling through the ground, determining the second, larger event to be the equivalent of an earthquake measuring 3.4 on the Richter scale.

All 320 men on duty at the pier died instantly, and 390 civilian and military personnel were injured, many seriously. Among the dead were five

Coast Guard personnel posted on board the fire barge. Afro-Americans killed totaled 202, and 233 were injured which accounted for 15% of all the African-Americans naval casualties during WW II. Naval personnel worked quickly to contain the fires and to prevent other explosions. Injuries were treated; those seriously injured were hospitalized, and uninjured servicemen were evacuated to nearby stations.

After the fires had been contained, there remained the gruesome task of cleaning up body parts and corpses that littered the bay and port. Most of the uninjured sailors volunteered to help clean up and rebuild the base. The men were all in a state of shock and nervous. Many of them inquired about obtaining a "30-day survivor's leave," some time given by the Navy to sailors who had survived a serious incident where the friends or shipmates had died; but no 30-day leaves were granted, not even to those who had been hospitalized with injuries. White officers, however, received the leave, causing a major grievance among the enlisted men.

A Naval Board of Inquiry was convened on July 21, 1944 to find out what happened. The official proceeding lasted 39 days and included interviews with witnesses who were officers, civilians and enlisted men. Ordnance experts were questioned as well as previous overseeing inspectors. Captain Kinne's posted division tonnage results come to light in the inquiry, but he stated that the competition to load the most tonnage did not make unsafe conditions and implied that junior officers who said so didn't know what they were talking about. Captain M. T. Kinne had served in the Navy from 1915 to 1922 and returned from civilian life to the Navy in 1941. Kinne had no training in the loading of munitions and almost no experience in handling them. White loading officers had not been trained in supervising enlisted personnel or handling munitions. From the top to the very bottom of the assigned military personnel, enlisted black or white at the Port Chicago Naval Magazine did not have the needed training to run the base.

A month after the explosion, continuing unsafe conditions inspired hundreds of servicemen to refuse to load munitions, an act known as the Port Chicago Mutiny. Fifty men called the "Port Chicago 50" were convicted of mutiny and sentenced to long prison terms. Forty-seven of the 50 were released in January 1946; the remaining three served additional months in prison.

Admiral Carleton Wright, Commander of the 12th Naval District, soon began implementing a plan to have two groups of white sailors load ammunition in rotation with black soldiers: one division of 100 men at Mare Island and another at Port Chicago. No plan was forwarded to use black officers to command the black sailors, and no plan included any form of desegregation. Wright sent a report of the incident to Washington, D.C. telling his superior officers that the men's "refusal to perform the required work arises from a mass fear arising out of the Port Chicago explosion." Wright's report was passed to President Roosevelt by the Secretary of the Navy James Forrestal who added his opinion that it was "mass fear" motivating the work stoppage. Forrestal told Roosevelt that white units of munitions were to be added to the rotation in order to avoid any semblance of discrimination against Negroes. Roosevelt forwarded a copy to his wife, Eleanor, knowing her ongoing advocacy of civil rights for African-Americans.

During and after the trial, questions were raised about the fairness and legality of the court-martial proceedings. Due to public pressure, the United States Navy reconvened the court martial in 1945. The court affirmed the guilt of the convicted men. Widespread publicity surrounding the case turned into *cause celebre* between African and white Americans. It and other race related Navy protests of 1944-1945 led the Navy to change its practices and initiate the desegregation of its forces beginning in February 1946. In 1944, the Port Chicago Naval Magazine National Memorial was dedicated to the lives lost in the disaster. Recently there has been some activity there honoring those who died there in the service of their country years ago.

The Navy asked Congress to give each victim's family $5,000. Representative John E. Rankin (D-MS) insisted the amount be $2,000 when he learned most of the dead were black men. Congress settled on $3,000 in compensation and interred what little remained of the victims in the local cemetery with the tombstones reading "Unknown, US Navy, 19 July 1944."

Years later on March 4, 1949, the heirs of 18 merchant seamen killed in the explosion were granted a total of $390,000 after gaining approval of their consent decrees in the United States District Court for the Northern District of California. Sounds rather familiar to us few still living WW II veterans and the thousands of family members of those Merchant Marines who have never gotten a penny of benefit from the US Congress since the war ended. We were considered to be civilians by the Navy. In this case it worked reliably for the heirs of the Merchant Mariner victims. Their case was tried in a civil court rather than a Military Tribunal. Many, many officers and I were sworn in as Naval Reserve officers, but that meant nothing unless we went on active duty on a Navy ship.

Invasion Plans

The invasion of Europe to defeat Germany and Italy in WW II required planning, personnel and materials on a scale never before seen in history. Planning required input and leadership from all the allies involved. Success required air, ground and Naval forces and the Merchant Marine. A mutual decision on where and when to invade took almost three years to resolve. Once landed, the Allied force than faced the logistical nightmare of supporting the invasion with armor, equipment, food, fuel, machinery, support personnel and transport. The War Shipping Administration V-4 Tugs manned by Merchant Mariners played a remarkable role in the success of the invasion.

Perry Adams remembers that the trip from the east coast to the UK in March, 1944, was the roughest trip he ever made in his life. "Several times we thought the damn ship was going to capsize." One day the weather was so bad that they had to turn around in the convoy lest the tugs could go down by the head. That is, they could come down on the backside of a huge wave and the ship would just continue on down. It wasn't likely since they were towing a barge, but for those tugs that were not towing anything it would be possible. Very little food was cooked due to the rolling and pitching, and some of the crewmen were afraid they would go down. The skipper ordered everyone to wear their life jackets 24/7. "We were attacked by U-boats three times during the trip when we were approaching the UK. The escorts said the subs fired torpedoes but did not hit anything." Army and Navy tugs worked with the WSA, War Shipping Administration, on big projects.

Germany began to fortify the coast of France by shifting troops, building bunkers, mining waters, installing impediments on the beaches, etc. The objective was a formidable one in keeping with the German design of having a fortress Europe. Any attempt by the allies to enter any of the captured ports would cause these ports to be destroyed, thus preventing allied entry.

They were well aware of the buildup in Great Britain and the certainty that an invasion would take place, but they believed Calais would be the best approach as it was the narrowest point in the English Channel. Other possible landing points were anticipated as diversions on the part of the Allies. There were three major disadvantages in selecting Normandy. One, there was no deep water there for a port. Two, with no port available, how would it be possible to equip the army once it landed. Three, conditions on the beaches were extremely treacherous. Surely these obstacles would make the invasion of Normandy unworkable, creating a mass slaughter of Allied troops. It did just that.

Leadership for Operation Neptune tug affairs was given to *Capt. Edmond Moran*, who was the perfect person for this task. Soon after the beginning of WW II, Moran became a consultant to the U.S. Maritime Commission. After Pearl Harbor, he resigned as President of Moran Towing & Transportation Co. in New York and reestablished his commission in the U.S. Navy. Michael Moran was born in Ireland in 1832, immigrated to the U.S. and began working as a mule driver on the Erie Canal. He saved his earnings and was able to purchase several barges. In 1869, he came to New York City and became a tugboat agent. Moran Towing quickly developed to a maritime prowess both nationally and internationally. That is probably still the case. As a project manager years ago, I used them to tow six of the world's largest power generating barges from the shipyard in Newport News, VA to NYC as quickly as possible to provide power for Con Edison. My top young field engineer was like me, a Merchant Mariner, and we did better than our GE contract schedule. When we got back to NYC, they mistakenly called us "heroes" for a day or two.

One of the first problems that Capt. Moran tackled was the need for a shipping container that could land on Normandy beaches at low tide. The solution lay in the use of New York City harbor floats and oil carrying barges, but first they had to be structured to withstand the rough conditions of the Atlantic Ocean while being shipped to England. The solution was to piggy back the two, thereby increasing their strength. As Perry Adams said, crossing the ocean to England on a tug was the worst condition he had ever seen in his whole long life. Can you imagine the sea sickness and vomiting those young barge crews must have suffered on a crossing?

Those V-4 tugs were to be civilian operated and carry a crew of 36 along with a Navy Armed Guard gun crew. Merchant Mariners were called civilians in those days despite cadet and officers training and officers having been sworn in as U. S. Naval Reserves. Moran Towing & Transportation received several congratulatory letters for their towing accomplishments, and Capt. Edmond J. Moran became Rear Admiral Moran. I once had a Moran as a fireman water tender on my watch on a T-2 tanker who said he was one of that well-known family but did not like his name being spelled or addressed as Moron.

Farallon's Armed Guard Commander Guido De Angelis BM1/c reports the Fallon's operation between April 19, 1944 and October 1, 1944:

This vessel has been operating in the English Channel area, operating between Lee-on-Solent and London via the Straits of Dover. From D-day on, our voyages were extended to Normandy, France. A total of ten block ships were taken over in three months. On each occasion back, this vessel would return to the UK with some disabled vessel. Among our tows were the Liberty John Truman and H. D. Blaskdell, the latter a troop ship. Both of these ships hit mines in route to France. Also towed back from France was the British freighter, Fort Yale, on August 23, 1944. This vessel was torpedoed off the Isle of Wight and had to be abandoned. It sank inside one half hour . . . On two occasions this vessel, both times at night, opened fire on hostile aircraft while at anchor off Arromanches, France . . . results unknown. A total of 22 trips were made through the Straits of Dover and on one occasion we witnessed a shelling from Pais de Calais while we were anchored in Dover.

Perry Adams writes about the Farallon: There was a bunch of old ships that were scuttled to form a breakwater in addition to the concrete blocks we towed over there from the UK. It took about 18 to 22 hours to make the run from the storage anchorage area near Lee-in-Solent in southern England to the Normandy beaches and drop off the concrete blocks. On the first trip over, we left the anchorage area with our concrete blocks before dark on the 5th of June. We reached the Normandy coast the next morning and anchored near a battleship that was firing its 15-inch guns. This was a sight to see. You could actually see the shells coming out from the end of the gun.

We were some three miles offshore and we saw what we believed were hundreds of dead soldiers floating in the water. It made you sick to see them. Our first reaction was to try to pick them out of the water, but our orders were not to do so as they might have explosives attached to them by the Germans. Later the crew discussed this and concluded that the chance of them having explosives attached was most unlikely, and we wished we had tried to pick them up as we sailed by. I think on later trips we would have picked them up. On one of our trips over we went to the British port which was further north than the American port. There was a Scotch detachment being discharged and taken unto the beaches. We could clearly hear them playing the bagpipes as they landed and marched up the beach. Just like a Hollywood movie. Of course by then the Germans had retreated some miles inland.

WW II came upon us and all of a sudden these old barges that had been placed in the bone yards and mud flats were called back to service. The German U-boats were sinking our ships faster than we could build them. The larger and faster ships were needed to maintain our shipping lanes and keep our troops overseas supplied with badly needed materials and our shores free from the enemy.

Again families answered the call to man those old and dilapidated barges. Most seamen tended to steer away from those old hulks and go after the safer ships that had modern conveniences most people were used to. Since the healthier and younger seamen steered clear of those barges, that left older seamen and those less healthy to the old ones. The families again began to play an important role in this war. They manned these vessels and did what was necessary. They moved the war materials to the ports to support the defense plants that built the war materials for our troops overseas. Our large merchant fleet transported these materials to the three continents where our troops were fighting and keeping our shores free from the Axis powers. U-boats would attack these small barges if they thought their cargo was large enough, and did.

Captain W. J. Publicover, master of the tug Farallon in June 1944, was given a Bronze Star Citation for meritorious service and courageous devotion to duty during the landing operations in Normandy, France.

Tugboats at D-day, Normandy

Not all maritime operations are carried out by the large freighters, liners and tankers. The WSA service fleet at the end of the war was composed of 48 seagoing tugs of the V4-M-82 designed by the Maritime Commission. Their big jobs have included the towing of battle-damaged and storm-damaged merchant vessels and Army and Navy combat ships to the nearest ports where repairs could be made. Since 1942, this fleet handled 784 tows involving 1,167 units which piled up a record of 1,893,200 miles of ocean expanses and through all sorts of weather conditions and enemy action. Their exploits won fame for the men who manned them, as with the ten tugs which were in the famous Mulberry operation on the Normandy beachhead. While these ten were at work in Europe, the balances were towing dry docks, floating repair ships and other non-self-propelled units from the U.S. to forward areas, principally in the Pacific. Coastwise tugs aided in the northeastern coal trade and towed large oil barges across the Gulf of Mexico.

Lester Ellison was promoted to Captain on a tug near the end of the war. Participating in the Normandy invasion was a particularly hazardous duty.

First, there was the matter of the explosive designed to scuttle ships. Then there were the Germans firing away at anything that moved in the harbor or on the beach. The danger of being struck by a floating mine was ever present. And there were activities that, because of the complexity and size of the invasion, couldn't go by "standard operating procedure." We were assigned to move a barge loaded with explosives to a beach that had not been cleared of mines. Luckily we carried out our assignment without mishap, but now I still think back to how deadly the Normandy invasion proved to be.

Purser/pharmacist *Perry Adams* served aboard two of the V-Tugboats (called Little Giants). I first joined Yaquina Head on November 1, 1943 and was transferred to the Fallon in January 1944. I sailed on her until May 1946, so I pretty well knew my way around the V-4 tugs. A couple of observations I would like to make. First, I came to the conclusion many years later that our German enemy submarines did not want to waste a big expensive torpedo on a little tugboat. In place of sinking us, they aimed at our tow which, in our case, twice sank a much larger and important ship than we were. Twice I witnessed the torpedo wake heading toward us, but in fact they both were aimed and did hit our tows – one a freighter we were towing back to the UK from Normandy and an LST we were towing back to the U.S. The LST was in our convoy coming home in December 1944. She broke down, and we picked her up and were continuing home not far from the Azores at the time she was torpedoed.

Another observation: The crews on the tugs were usually young, right out of the training bases. The reason is that few experienced old salts cared for the rough riding and cramped quarters of the V-4s. (I have spoken recently by phone with Perry Adams and Les Ellison. They feel their ages, but both are very talkative and wish us the best results with our MM publishing efforts.)

Robert Pribbenow, a seaman aboard the V-4 tug Farallon, stated that so many who went to Normandy were called heroes. When I saw the bodies at Omaha Beach, they were the heroes. Perry Adams tells about the Farallon leaving the U.S. in March 1944, towing three steel railroad bridges. When they go to the UK, the "Limies" (an old time American nickname for English sailors, who were given limes at sea to avoid the dreaded scurvy, a disease of the teeth, mouth and gums) converted them to floating docks. They looked like a large upside down table with legs sticking up into the air. Actually the legs went down to the bottom of the ocean. That held the dock in position, but the dock itself floated up and down on those legs with the 13 to 18 foot tides on the channel.

Those V-4 tugs were active on the West Coast and the Pacific islands, and they had Navy crews on board.
Navy Armed Guard Commander *Guido DeAngelis* reported the following developments aboard the tug MV Farallon:

> *We started the journey back to the States in rather rough weather. Our convoy was composed of mostly tugs, LCIs, LSTs and destroyers. Most of them were disabled and were being towed. This vessel started out light; however, after being underway three days, our sister ship, the Moose Park, broke away from her tow and this tug took over the job of towing LST-359. Upon picking up this tow, we proceeded into a convoy again. Weather conditions vastly improved.*

On December 20, 1944, the special towing convoy which had been formed with the escort of Task Group 27.4 was moving slowly through the sea. A report of enemy action had come in. Two short-base aircraft were conducting a search in the general area northward of the convoy, presumably to locate a submarine reported 100 miles away by the Admiralty. The convoy was doing 8.5 knots. Perry Adams aboard the MV says:

> *I was on the after section of the bridge deck of the MV Farallon at about midmorning. The sky was mostly clear and sunny. The temperature was probably in the mid-50s. A slight breeze was blowing*

with an occasional white cap breaking. The day could be described as an almost perfect day from a sailor's point of view.

The convoy was moving in a westerly direction a few hundred miles off the coast of the Azores Islands heading home to the Eastern coast of the United States.

A few minutes after 1030 hours, the chief radio officer, *William L. Smith*, and Perry were looking over the port (left) side when they saw a torpedo streaming toward them. Perry jumped to ring the general alarm button. The bridge watch officer and bow lookout saw the torpedo and tried to steer the Farallon out of its line of travel, and was lucky again. (Adams and "Smitty" at almost the same moment were standing in the same place on their ship on August 23, when a torpedo missed them and sank the SS Fort Yale.) The torpedo hit port side of their tow, causing a huge explosion and making a gaping hole all the way down below the water line.

Within a few minutes the convoy escort USS Fogg came racing by, and Perry Adams still remembers a bullhorn message from her saying, "I will take care of this." At that point in time the Farallon was dead in the water. The USS Fogg made a turn and came up on the starboard (right) side of the Farallon. The submarine's periscope was only 50 feet away and their bow gun could not be depressed low enough to hit it. But the USS Fogg, 500 to 700 yards away, had turned her stern to face the Farallon and was preparing to launch depth charges when a torpedo hit the stern of the USS Fogg. The submarine's captain seized the opportunity to lower the periscope and disappear; however, before it disappeared, one of the cooks got off several shots of Irish potatoes in frustration.

About 1,000 American Mariners in Operation Mulberry sailed in more than 20 obsolete merchant ships to be sunk as artificial harbors on the southern French beachheads. More than 2,600 merchant ships were involved in the June 6, 1944 invasion.

From Mr. J. Don Horton on his barge life with his family on the east coast: At the outset of the war, women tried to get work in the U.S. Merchant Marine. They were dealt a death blow by War Shipping Administrator Adm. Emory S. Land who stated that there was no place in the Merchant Marine for women. By this order the US Coast Guard refused to document women who served. They served anyway and did what was asked of them without any recognition of their work. They served on many barges as well as vessels, mostly as cooks and mess men. They were paid salaries and Social Security taxes were taken from their wages. Efforts to gain status as seamen by the women were met with stern denial from the various captains of ports up and down the coast.

War in the Pacific

On December 7, 1941, Japanese forces attacked the US Pacific Fleet at Pearl Harbor, Hawaii. The attack crippled much of the US battleship fleet and precipitated an open and formal state of war between the two nations. The initial goals of the Japanese leaders were to neutralize the US Navy, seize the possessions rich in natural resources and establish strategic military bases to defend Japan's empire in the Pacific Ocean and Asia. To further those goals, Japanese forces captured the Philippines, Thailand, Malaya, Singapore, Burma, the Dutch East Indies, Wake Island, Gilbert Islands, New Britain and Guam.

The Japanese Navy never targeted shipping in the Pacific. Hundreds of merchant ships and thousands of mariners shuttled all the wartime needs of the fighting men to the Pacific shores where they risked unloading at island beachheads and where well more than 40 ships were sunk. Countless other vessels, mostly Liberty ships, were damaged by aircraft, kamikazes, artillery and torpedoes while taking part in being in every combat area.

Lt. General Alexander A. Vandegrift, Commandant of the Marine Corps: "The men and ships of the Merchant Marine have participated in every landing operation by the United States Marine Corps from Guadalcanal to Iwo Jima— and we know they will be at hand with supplies and equipment when every amphibious force hits the beaches of Japan itself."

The *Admiral Halstead* was in Port Darwin, Australia in February 19, 1941 with 14,000 barrels of aviation octane gasoline. The Japanese launched their first heavy air raid that damaged every vessel in the harbor except the *Admiral Halstead*. Military authorities ordered the crew to leave the ship. For days, six of her crew volunteered to re-board her each morning to take her away from the docks, and each night bring her back and turn on her cargo pumps to discharge the precious fuel into shore side tanks. Port Darwin was the only Australian port that the Japanese bombers could reach and return back to their base. The town was vacated except for a few military. We Americans hauled fuel from the Abadan, Iran refinery with our T-2 to Port Darwin after the Japs were pushed back. On the last of our trips the Sergeant in Charge was still at the jetty. I greeted him with, "The war's over and you didn't go home." He explained that his younger brother wanted out of the army quickly. Australian military regulations allowed him to serve days of active duty for his kid brother's service time.

In the October 1944 Battle for the Philippines, merchant ships delivered 30,000 American and Allied troops and 500,000 tons of supplies to Leyte during the invasion. They shot down more than 100 enemy planes during the almost continuous air attacks. During the Mindoro invasion more Merchant Mariners lost their lives than did all the other armed services combined. Sixty-eight Mariners and Armed Guard on the SS *John Burke* and 71 on the *Lewis E. Dyche* disappeared, along with ammunition-laden ships, due to kamikaze attacks.

General Douglas MacArthur commented on the Mindoro Invasion: "I have ordered them off their ships and into fox holes when their ships became untenable under attack. They displayed a high caliber of efficiency and courage throughout the entire campaign in the Southwest Pacific area. I hold no branch in higher esteem than the Merchant Marine."

Merchant ships delivered many of the 180,000 troops and more than a million tons of supplies during the invasion of Okinawa while under attack from 2,000 kamikazes and other aircraft.

Casualties:
U.S. -- 7,100 dead, four captured, 29 ships lost, 615 aircraft lost.
Japan -- 31,000 dead, 1,000 captured, 38 ships lost, 683-880 aircraft lost.

With the death of Adolf Hitler (Schiklgruber), "Der Fuhrer," and his mistress, Eva Braun, in Berlin by suicide, after marrying April 30, 1945, it was time for the planned movement for our forces in the east to move west and destroy the Japanese forces in their homeland.

The invasion of the main island of the Empire of Japan would be tougher than any other invasion in the war to date. The US forces in the Pacific had suffered 300,000 battle casualties up to July 1, 1945. An assault was predicted to kill and wound a million or more and involve close to five million American soldiers, sailors, marines, coast guard and merchant mariners. Convoys carrying troops, supplies and all the wartime needs to landings on the Japanese Islands coast lines would have to cross hundreds of miles of ocean.

Fortunately, in the early days of August 1945, with our dropping "atomic bombs" on Hiroshima and Nagasaki, which killed 210,000, the greatest war on earth, WW II, ended in an unconditional Japanese surrender.

After the surrender, Japanese units continued in various areas throughout the Pacific. The Merchant Marine was given the job of transporting the surrendered armies back to Japan.

US Merchant Mariners also had to return the tired, wounded and dead US troops home to the States. They had to bring in replacement forces and supplies for the Occupation. Arms and bombs had to be returned to the USA. In December 1945, the War Shipping Administration listed 1,200 sailings - 400 more than the busiest month of the previous four years.

Merchant Mariners on their Liberty ships, WW I vintage "Hog Islanders," and anything else that floated took part in every invasion of WW II. Many Liberties had invasion barges with temporary accommodations for 200 troops. These were ready to be lowered from the rigging at beaches under enemy fire.

Guadalcanal Campaign

The Guadalcanal Campaign, also known as the Battle of Guadalcanal and code named Operation Watchtower by Allied forces, was a military campaign fought between August 7, 1942 and February 9, 1943 on and around the island of Guadalcanal in the Pacific theater of World War II. It was the first major offensive by Allied forces against the Empire of Japan.

On August 7, 1942, Allied forces, predominantly American, landed on the islands of Guadalcanal, Tulagi, and Florida in the southern Solomon Islands with the objective of denying their use by the Japanese to threaten the supply and communication routes between the U.S., Australia, and New Zealand. The Allies also intended to use Guadalcanal and Tulagi as bases to support a campaign to eventually capture or neutralize the major Japanese base at Rabaul on New Britain. The Allies overwhelmed the outnumbered Japanese defenders, who had occupied the islands since May 1942, and captured Tulagi and Florida, as well as an airfield (later named Henderson Field in honor of Lofton R. Henderson, a Marine aviator who was killed during the Battle of Midway) that was under construction on Guadalcanal. Powerful U.S. naval forces supported the landings.

Surprised by the Allied offensive, the Japanese made several attempts between August and November 1942 to retake Henderson Field. Three major land battles, seven large naval battles (five nighttime surface actions and two carrier battles), and continual, almost daily aerial battles culminated in the decisive Naval Battle of Guadalcanal in early November 1942, in which the last Japanese attempt to bombard Henderson Field from the sea and land with enough troops to retake it was defeated. In December 1942, the Japanese abandoned further efforts to retake Guadalcanal and evacuated their remaining forces on February 7, 1943 in the face of an offensive by the US Army's XIV Corps, conceding the island to the Allies.

Action in the Pacific

The Liberty Ship S.S.John W. Gouch after being hit by a torpedo from a Japanese plane while discharging cargo at Guadalcanal October 1943. All hands abandon ship as fire quickly spread. 2 crew members were lost.

Two attempts by the Japanese to continue their strategic initiative and offensively extend their outer defensive perimeter in the south and central Pacific to where they could threaten Australia and Hawaii or the US West Coast were thwarted at the naval battles of Coral Sea and Midway respectively. Coral Sea was a tactical stalemate, but a strategic Allied victory which became clear only much later. Midway was not only the Allies' first clear major victory against the Japanese, it significantly reduced the offensive capability of Japan's carrier forces, but did not change their offensive mind-set for several crucial months.

The Allies chose the Solomon Islands (a protectorate of Great Britain), specifically the southern Solomon Islands of Guadalcanal, Tulagi and Florida Island, as the first target. The Imperial Japanese Navy had occupied Tulagi in May 1942 and had constructed a seaplane base nearby.

The Allied plan to invade the southern Solomons was conceived by U.S. Admiral Ernest King, Commander in Chief, United States Fleet. He proposed the offensive to deny the use of the island by the Japanese as bases to threaten the supply routes between the United States and Australia and to use them as starting points. With Roosevelt's tacit consent, King also advocated the invasion of Guadalcanal. Because the United States supported Great Britain's proposal that priorities be given to defeating Germany before Japan, the Pacific theater had to compete for personnel and resources with the European theater. Therefore US Army General George C. Marshall opposed King's proposed campaign and asked who would command the operation. King replied that the Navy and Marines would carry out the operation by themselves and instructed Admiral Chester Nimitz to proceed with the preliminary planning. King eventually won the argument with Marshall and the invasion went ahead with the backing of the Combined Joint Chiefs (CJCS).

The CJCS ordered for 1942-43 Pacific objectives: that Guadalcanal would be carried out in conjunction with an Allied offensive in New Guinea under Douglas MacArthur, to capture the Admiralty Islands and the Bismarck Archipelago, including the major Japanese base at Rabaul. The directive held that the eventual goal was the American re-conquest of the Philippines. The U.S. Joint Chiefs of Staff created the South Pacific Theater, with Vice Admiral Robert L. Ghormley taking command on June 19, 1942, to direct the offensive in the Solomons Admiral Chester Nimitz, based at Pearl Harbor, was designated an overall Allied commander in chief for Pacific forces.

Task Force

In preparation for the offensive in May 1942, the U.S. Marine Major General *Alexander Vandegrift* was ordered to move his 1st Marine Division from the United States to New Zealand.

At first, the Allied offensive was planned just for Tulagi and the Santa Cruz Islands, omitting Guadalcanal. After Allied reconnaissance discovered the Japanese airfield construction efforts on Guadalcanal, its capture was added to the plan and the Santa Cruz operation was (eventually) dropped. The Japanese were aware, via signals intelligence, of the large-scale movement of Allied forces in the South Pacific area but concluded that the Allies were reinforcing Australia and perhaps Port Moresby in New Guinea.

General Vandegrift led the 16,000 allied (primarily U.S. Marine) infantry earmarked for the landings. The troops sent to Guadalcanal were fresh from military training and armed with issue bolt action '03 Springfield rifles and a meager 10-day supply of ammunition. Due to the necessity of getting them into battle quickly, the operation planners had reduced their supplies from a 90-day supply to only 60 days. The troops of the 1st Marine Division began referring to the coming battle as "Operation Shoestring."

Landings

Bad weather allowed the Allied expeditionary force to arrive in the vicinity of Guadalcanal unseen by the Japanese on the morning of August 7 and take the defenders by surprise. The landing force split into two groups, with one group assaulting Guadalcanal, and the other Tulagi, Florida, and nearby islands. Allied warships bombarded the invasion beaches while U.S. carrier aircraft bombed Japanese positions on the target islands and destroyed 15 Japanese seaplanes at their base near Tulagi.

With some difficulty, the Marines secured all three islands; Tulagi on August 8, and Gavutu and Tanambogo by August 9. The Japanese defenders were killed almost to the last man, while the Marines suffered 122 killed.

During the landing operations on August 7 and August 8, Japanese naval aircraft based at Rabaul, attacked the Allied amphibious forces several times, setting afire the transport USS *George F. Elliot* (which sank two days later) and heavily damaging the destroyer USS *Jarvis*. In the air attacks over the two days, the Japanese lost 36 aircraft, while the U.S. lost 19, both in combat and to accidents, including 14 carrier fighters.

Battle of Savo Island

One night, as the transports unloaded, two groups of screening Allied cruisers and destroyers, under the command of British Rear Admiral Victor Crutchley, were surprised and defeated by a Japanese force of seven cruisers and one destroyer from the 8th Fleet based at Rabaul and Kavieng and commanded by Japanese Vice Admiral Gunichi Mikawa. In the Battle of Savo Island one Australian and three American cruisers were sunk and one American cruiser and two destroyers were damaged. The Japanese suffered moderate damage to one cruiser.

Initial Operations

The 11,000 Marines on Guadalcanal initially concentrated on forming a loose defensive perimeter around Lunga Point and the airfield, moving the landed supplies within the perimeter, and finishing the airfield. In four days of intense effort, the supplies were moved from the landing beach into dispersed dumps within the perimeter. Work began on the airfield immediately, mainly using captured Japanese equipment. On August 12, the airfield was named Henderson Field after Lofton R. Henderson, a marine aviator who was killed during the Battle of

Midway. By August 18, the airfield was ready for operation. Five days worth of food had been landed from the merchant marine transports, which, along with captured Japanese provisions, gave the Marines a total of 14 days worth of food. To conserve supplies, the troops were limited to two meals per day.

Allied troops encountered a severe strain of dysentery soon after the landings, with one in five Marines afflicted by mid-August. Tropical diseases would affect the fighting strengths of both sides throughout the campaign. Although some of the Korean construction workers surrendered to the Marines, most of the remaining Japanese and Korean personnel gathered just west of the Lunga perimeter on the west bank of the Matanikau River and subsisted mainly on coconuts.

On the evening of August 12, a 25-man U.S. Marine patrol, led by Lieutenant Colonel *Frank Goettge* and primarily consisting of intelligence personnel, landed by boat west of the Lunga perimeter, between Point Cruz and the Matanikau River, on a reconnaissance mission with a secondary objective of contacting a group of Japanese troops that U.S. forces believed might be willing to surrender. Soon after the patrol landed, a nearby platoon of Japanese naval troops attacked and almost completely wiped out the Marine patrol.

In response, on August 19, Vandegrift sent three companies of the U.S. 5th Marine Regiment to attack the Japanese troop concentration west of the Matanikau. One company attacked across the sandbar at the mouth of the Matanikau River while another crossed the river 1,000 meters (1,100 yd) inland and attacked the Japanese forces located in Matanikau villages. The third landed by boat further west and attacked Kokumbuna villages. After briefly occupying the two villages, the three Marine companies returned to the Lunga perimeter, having killed about 65 Japanese soldiers while losing four.

Battle of the Tenaru

In response to the Allied landings on Guadalcanal, the Japanese Imperial General Headquarters assigned the Imperial Japanese Army's (IJA) 17th Army, a corps-sized command based at Rabaul and under the command of Lieutenant General Harukichi Hyakutake, the task of retaking Guadalcanal. The army was to be supported by Japanese naval units, including the Combined Fleet. The 28th (Ichiki) Infantry Regiment, under the command of Colonel Kiyonao Ichiki, was on board transport ships near Guam. The different units began to move toward Guadalcanal via Truk and Rabaul immediately, but Ichiki's regiment, being the closest, arrived in the area first. A "First Element" of Ichiki's unit, consisting of about 917 soldiers, landed from destroyers at Taivu Point, east of the Lunga perimeter, after midnight on August 19, then made a 9-mile (14 km) night march west toward the Marine perimeter.

Underestimating the strength of Allied forces on Guadalcanal, Ichiki's unit conducted a nighttime frontal assault on Marine positions at Alligator Creek (often called the "Hu River" on the U.S. Marine maps) on the east side of the Lunga perimeter in the early morning hours of August 21. Ichiki's assault was defeated with heavy Japanese losses in what became known as the Battle of Tenaru. After daybreak, the Marine units counterattacked Ichiki's surviving troops, killing many more of them. The dead included Ichiki, though it has been claimed that he committed seppuku after realizing the magnitude of his defeat, rather than dying in combat. In total, all but 128 of the original 917 members of the Ichiki Regiment's First Element were killed.

Battle of the Eastern Solomons

As the Tenaru battle was ending, more Japanese reinforcements were already on their way. Three slow transports departed from Truk on August 16 carrying the remaining 1,400 soldiers from Ichiki's (28th) Infantry Regiment plus 500 naval marines from the 5th Yokosuka Special Naval Landing Force.

The transports were guarded by 13 warships that were commanded by Japanese Rear Admiral Raizo Tanaka, who planned to land the troops on Guadalcanal on August 24. To cover the landings of these troops and provide support for the operation to retake Henderson Field from Allied forces, Yamamoto directed Chuichi Nagumo to sortie with a carrier force from Truk on August 21 and head toward the southern Solomon Islands.

Simultaneously, three U.S. carrier task forces under Fletcher approached Guadalcanal to counter the Japanese offensive efforts. On August 24 and 25, the two carrier forces fought the Battle of the Eastern Solomons, which resulted in both fleets retreating from the area after taking some damage, with the Japanese losing one light aircraft carrier. Tanaka's convoy, after suffering heavy damage during the battle from an air attack by CAF aircraft from Henderson Field, including the sinking of one of the transports, was forced to divert to the Shortland Islands in the northern Solomons in order to transfer the surviving troops to destroyers for later delivery to Guadalcanal.

Air Battles Over Henderson Field and Strengthening of the Lunga Defenses

Throughout August, small numbers of U.S. aircraft and their crews continued to arrive at Guadalcanal. By the end of August, 64 aircraft of various types were stationed at Henderson Field. On September 3, the commander of 1ST Marine Aircraft Wing, U. S. Marine Brigadier General *Roy S. Geiger*, arrived with his staff and took command of all air operations at Henderson Field. Air battles between the Allied aircraft at Henderson and Japanese bombers and fighters from Rabaul continued almost daily. Between August 26 and September 5, the U. S. lost about 15 aircraft while the Japanese lost approximately 19 aircraft.

More than half of the downed U.S. aircrews were rescued while most of the Japanese aircrews were never recovered. The eight-hour round trip flight from Rabaul to Guadalcanal, about 1,120 miles (1,800 km) total, seriously hampered Japanese efforts to establish air superiority over Henderson Field. Australian coast watchers on Bougainville and New Georgia islands were often able to provide Allied forces on Guadalcanal with advance notice of inbound Japanese air strikes, allowing the U.S. fighters time to take off and position themselves to attack the Japanese bombers and fighters as they approached the island. Thus, the Japanese air forces were slowly losing a war of attrition in the skies above Guadalcanal.

During this time, Vandegrift continued to direct efforts to strengthen and improve the defenses of the Lunga perimeter. Between August 21 and September 3, he relocated three Marine battalions, including the 1st Raider Battalion, under *Merritt S. Edson* (Edson's Raiders), and the 1st Parachute Battalion from Tulagi and Gavutu to Guadalcanal. These units added about 1,500 troops to Vandegrift's original 11,000 men defending Henderson Field. The 1st Parachute Battalion, which had suffered heavy casualties in the Battle of Tulagi and Gavutu-Tanambogo in August, was placed under Edson's command.

The other relocated battalion, the 1st Battalion, 5th Marine Regiment (1/5), was landed by boat west of the Matanikau near Kokumbuna village on August 27 with the mission of attacking Japanese units in the area, much as in the first Matanikau action of August 19. In this case, however, the Marines were impeded by difficult terrain, hot sun, and well-emplaced Japanese defenses. The next morning, the Marines found that the Japanese defenders had departed during the night, so the Marines returned to the Lunga perimeter by boat. Losses in this action were 20 Japanese and three Marines killed.

Small Allied naval merchant marine convoys arrived at Guadalcanal on August 23, August 29, September 1, and September 8 to provide the Marines at Lunga with more food, ammunition, aircraft fuel, and aircraft technicians. The September 1 convoy also brought 392 construction engineers to maintain and improve Henderson Field.

Tokyo Express

The damage done to Tanaka's convoy during the Battle of the Eastern Solomons caused the Japanese to reconsider trying to deliver more troops to Guadalcanal by slow transport. Instead, the ships carrying Kawaguchi's soldiers were sent to Rabaul. From there, the Japanese planned to deliver Kawaguchi's men to Guadalcanal by destroyers staging through a Japanese naval base in the Shortland Islands. The Japanese destroyers were usually able to make round trips down "The Slot" (New Georgia Sound) to Guadalcanal and back in a single night throughout the campaign, minimizing their exposure to Allied air attack; they became known as the "Tokyo Express" to Allied forces and were labeled "Rat Transportation" by the Japanese. Delivering the troops in this manner, however, prevented most of the heavy equipment and supplies, such as heavy artillery, vehicles, and much food and ammunition, from being transported to Guadalcanal with them. In addition, this activity tied up destroyers the IJN desperately needed for commerce defense. Either inability or unwillingness prevented Allied naval commanders from challenging Japanese naval forces at night, so the Japanese controlled the seas around the Solomon Islands during nighttime. However, any Japanese ship remaining within range of the aircraft at Henderson Field during the daylight hours, about 200 miles (320 km), was in great danger from air attack. This tactical situation existed for the next several months of the campaign.

Battle of Edson's Ridge

U.S. Marine Lieutenant Colonel Merritt A. Edson, along with Colonel *Gerald C. Thomas*, Vandegrift's operations officer, correctly believed that the Japanese attack would come at a narrow, grassy, 1,000 yards-long (910 m), coral ridge that ran parallel to the Lunga River located just south of Henderson Field. The ridge, called Lunga Ridge, offered a natural avenue of approach to the airfield, commanded the surrounding area and, at that time, was almost undefended. On September 11 the 840 men of Edson's battalion were deployed onto and around the ridge.

On the night of September 12, Kawaguchi's 1st Battalion attacked the Raiders between the Lunga River and ridge, forcing one Marine company to fall back to the ridge before the Japanese halted their attack for the night. The next night Kawaguchi faced Edson's 830 Raiders with 3,000 troops of his brigade plus an assortment of light artillery. The Japanese attack began just after nightfall with Kawaguchi's 1st Battalion assaulting Edson's right flank just to the west of the ridge. After breaking through the Marine lines the battalion's assault was eventually stopped by Marine units guarding the northern part of the ridge.

Reinforcement

As the Japanese regrouped west of the Matanikau, the U.S. forces concentrated on shoring up and strengthening their Lunga defenses. On September 14 Vandegrift moved another battalion, the 3rd Battalion, 2nd Marine Regiment (3/2), from Tulagi to Guadalcanal. On September 18 an Allied naval convoy delivered 4,157 men from the 3rd Provisional Marine Brigade (the 7th Marine Regiment plus a battalion from the 11th Marine Regiment and some additional support units), 137 vehicles, tents, aviation fuel, ammunition, rations, and engineering equipment to Guadalcanal. These crucial reinforcements allowed Vandegrift, beginning on September 19, to establish an unbroken line of defense around the Lunga perimeter. While covering this convoy, the aircraft carrier USS *Wasp* was sunk by the Japanese submarine *I-19* southeast of Guadalcanal, temporarily leaving only one Allied aircraft carrier (USS *Hornet*) in operation in the South Pacific area. Vandegrift also made some changes in the senior leadership of his combat units, transferring off the island several officers who did not meet his performance standards and promoting junior officers who had proven themselves to take their places. One of these was the recently promoted Colonel Merritt Edson who was placed in command of the 5th Marine Regiment.

A lull occurred in the air war over Guadalcanal, with no Japanese air raids occurring between September 14 and September 27 due to bad weather, during which both sides reinforced their respective air units. The Japanese delivered 85 fighters and bombers to their air units at Rabaul while the U.S. brought 23 fighters and attack aircraft to Henderson Field. On September 20 the Japanese counted 117 total aircraft at Rabaul while the Allies tallied 71 aircraft at Henderson Field. The war resumed with a Japanese air raid on Guadalcanal on September 27 which was contested by U.S. Navy and Marine fighters from Henderson Field.

The Japanese immediately began to prepare for their next attempt to recapture Henderson Field.

Actions Along the Matanikau

Vandegrift and his staff were aware that Kawaguchi's troops had retreated to the area west of the Matanikau and that numerous groups of Japanese stragglers were scattered throughout the area between the Lunga Perimeter and the Matanikau River. Vandegrift, therefore, decided to conduct another series of small unit operations around the Matanikau Valley. The purpose of these operations was to mop up the scattered groups of Japanese troops east of the Matanikau and to keep the main body of Japanese soldiers off-balance to prevent them from consolidating their positions so close to the Marine defenses at Lunga Point.

The first U.S. Marine operation and attempt to attack Japanese forces west of the Matanikau, conducted between September 23 and 27 by elements of three U.S. Marine battalions, were repulsed by Kawaguchi's troops under Akinosuke Oka's local command. During the action, three Marine companies were surrounded by Japanese forces near Point Cruz west of the Matanikau, took heavy losses, and barely escaped with assistance from the destroyer USS *Monssen* (DD-436) and landing craft manned by U.S. Coast Guard personnel.

In the second action between October 6 and 9, a larger force of Marines successfully crossed the Matanikau River, attacked newly landed Japanese forces from the 2ⁿᵈ Infantry Division under the command of generals Masao Maruyama and Yumio Nasu, and inflicted heavy losses on the Japanese 4ᵗʰ Infantry Regiment. The second action forced the Japanese to retreat from their positions east of the Matanikau and hindered Japanese preparations for their planned major offensive on the U.S. Lunga defenses.

Battle of Cape Esperance

Millard F. Harmon, commander of the United States Army forces in the South Pacific, convinced Ghormley that U.S. Marine forces on Guadalcanal needed to be reinforced immediately if the Allies were to successfully defend the island from the next expected Japanese offensive. Thus, on October 8, the 2,837 men of the 164ᵗʰ Infantry Regiment from the U.S. Army's American Division boarded ships at New Caledonia for the trip to Guadalcanal with a projected arrival date of October 13. To protect the transports carrying the 164ᵗʰ to Guadalcanal, Ghormley ordered Task Force 64, consisting of four cruisers and five destroyers under U.S. Rear Admiral Norman Scott, to intercept and combat any Japanese ships that approached Guadalcanal and threatened the arrival of the transport convoy.

Just before midnight, Scott's warships detected Goto's force on radar near the entrance to the strait between Savo Island and Guadalcanal. Scott's force was in a position to cross the T of Goto's unsuspecting formation. Opening fire, Scott's warships sank one of Goto's cruisers and one of his destroyers, heavily damaging another cruiser, mortally wounded Goto, and forced the rest of Goto's warships to abandon the bombardment mission and retreat. During the exchange of gunfire, one of Scott's destroyers was sunk and one cruiser and another destroyer were heavily damaged. In the meantime, the Japanese supply convoy successfully completed unloading at Guadalcanal and began its return journey without being discovered by Scott's force. Later on the morning of October 12, four Japanese destroyers from the supply convoy turned back to assist Goto's retreating, damaged warships. Air attacks by CAF aircraft from Henderson Field sank two of these destroyers later that day. The convoy of U.S. Army troops reached Guadalcanal as scheduled the next day and successfully delivered its cargo and passengers to the island.

Battleship Bombardment of Henderson Field

In spite of the U.S. victory off Cape Esperance, the Japanese continued with plans and preparations for their large offensive scheduled for later in October. The Japanese decided to risk a one-time departure from their usual practice of only using fast warships to deliver their men and material to the island. On October 13, a convoy comprising six cargo ships with eight screening destroyers departed the Shortland Islands for Guadalcanal. The convoy carried 4,500 troops from the 16th and 230th Infantry Regiments, some naval marines, two batteries of heavy artillery, and one company of tanks.

To protect the approaching convoy from attack by CAF aircraft, Yamamoto sent two battleships from Truk to bombard Henderson Field. At 1:33 on October 14, *Kongo* and *Haruna,* escorted by one light cruiser and nine destroyers, reached Guadalcanal and opened fire on Henderson Field from a distance of 16,000 meters (17,500 yd). Over the next one hour and 23 minutes, the two battleships fired 973 14-inch (356 mm) shells into the Lunga perimeter, most of them falling in and around the 2,200 meters (2,400 yd) square area of the airfield. Many of the shells were fragmentation shells, specifically designed to destroy land targets. The bombardment heavily damaged both runways, burned almost all of the available aviation fuel, destroyed 48 of the CAF's 90 aircraft, and killed 41 men, including six CAF pilots. The battleship force immediately returned to Truk.

In spite of the heavy damage, Henderson personnel were able to restore one of the runways to operational condition within a few hours. Seventeen SBDs and 20 Wildcats at Espiritu Santo were quickly flown to Henderson and U. S. Army and Marine transport aircraft began to shuttle aviation gasoline from Espiritu Santo to Guadalcanal. Now aware of the approach of the large Japanese reinforcement convoy, the U. S. desperately sought some way to interdict the convoy before it could reach Guadalcanal. Using fuel drained from destroyed aircraft and from a cache in the nearby jungle, the CAF attacked the convoy twice on the 14th, but caused no damage.

The Japanese convoy reached Tassafaronga on Guadalcanal at midnight on October 14 and began unloading. Throughout the day of October 15, a string of CAF aircraft from Henderson bombed and strafed the unloading convoy, destroying three of the cargo ships. The remainder of the convoy departed that night, having unloaded all of the troops and about two-thirds of the supplies and equipment. Several Japanese heavy cruisers also bombarded Henderson on the nights of October 14 and 15, destroying a few additional CAF aircraft, but failing to cause significant damage to the airfield.

Battle for Henderson Field

Between October 1 and October 17, the Japanese delivered 15,000 troops to Guadalcanal, giving Hyakutake 20,000 total troops to employ for his planned offensive. Because of the loss of their positions on the east side of the Matanikau, the Japanese decided that an attack on the U. S. defenses along the coast would be prohibitively difficult. Therefore, Hyakutake decided that the main thrust of his planned attack would be from south of Henderson Field. His 2nd Division (augmented by troops from the 38th Division), under Lieutenant General Masao Maruyama and comprising 7,000 soldiers in three infantry regiments of three battalions each, was ordered to march through the jungle and attack the American defenses from the south near the east bank of the Lunga River. The date of the attack was set for October 22, then changed to October 23. To distract the Americans from the planned attack from the south, Hyakutake's heavy artilleries plus five battalions of infantry (about 2,900 men) under Major General Tadashi Sumiyoshi were to attack American defenses from the west along the coastal corridor. The Japanese estimated that there were 10,000 American troops on the island, when in fact there were about 23,000.

On October 12, a company of Japanese engineers began to break a trail, called the "Maruyama Road," from the Matanikau toward the southern portion of the U. S. Lunga perimeter. The 15 miles (24 km) long trail traversed some of the most difficult terrain on Guadalcanal, including numerous rivers and streams, deep, muddy ravines, steel ridges, and dense jungle. Between October 16 and October 18, the 2nd Division began their march along the Maruyama Road.

U.S. Marine and Army units armed with rifles, machine guns, mortars, artillery, including direct canister fire from 37 mm antitank guns "wrought terrible carnage" on the Japanese. A few small groups of Japanese broke through the American defenses, but were all hunted down and killed over the next several days. More than 15,000 of Maruyama's troops were killed in the attacks while the Americans lost about 60 killed. Over the same two days American aircraft from Henderson Field defended against attacks by Japanese aircraft and ships, destroying 14 aircraft and sinking a light cruiser.

In total the Japanese lost 2,200 - 3,000 troops in the battle while the Americans lost around 80.

Battle of the Santa Cruz Islands

The two opposing carrier forces confronted each other on the morning of October 26, in what became known as the Battle of the Santa Cruz Islands. After an exchange of carrier air attacks, Allied surface ships were forced to retreat from the battle area with the loss of one carrier sunk (*Hornet*) and another (*Enterprise*) heavily damaged. The participating Japanese carrier forces, however, also retired because of high aircraft and aircrew losses and significant damage to two carriers. Although an apparent tactical victory for the Japanese in terms of ships sunk and damaged, the loss by the Japanese of many irreplaceable veteran aircrews provided a long-term strategic advantage for the Allies, whose aircrew losses in the battle were relatively low. The Japanese carriers played no further significant role in the campaign.

November Land Actions

In order to exploit the victory in the Battle for Henderson Field, Vandegrift sent six Marine battalions, later joined by one U. S. Army battalion, on an offensive west of the Matanikau. The operation was commanded by Merritt Edson and its goal was to capture Kokumbona, headquarters of the 17th Army, west of Point Cruz. Defending the Point Cruz areas were Japanese army troops from the 4th Infantry Regiment commanded by Nomasu Nakaguma. The 4th Infantry was severely under strength because of battle damage, tropical disease, and malnutrition.

At Koli Point early in the morning November 3, five Japanese destroyers delivered 300 army troops to support Shoji and his troops who were en route to Koli Point after the Battle for Henderson Field. Having learned of the planned landing, Vandegrift sent a battalion of Marines under Herman H. Hanneken to intercept the Japanese at Koli. Soon after the landing, the Japanese soldiers encountered and drove Hanneken's battalion back toward the Lunga perimeter. In response, Vandegrift ordered Puller's Marine battalion plus two of the 164th infantry battalion, along with Hanneken's battalion, to move toward Koli Point to attack the Japanese forces there.

As the American troops began to move, Shoji and his soldiers began to arrive at Koli Point. Beginning on November 8, the American troops attempted to encircle Shoji's forces at Gavaga Creek near Koli Point. Meanwhile, Hyakutake ordered Shoji to abandon his positions at Koli and rejoin Japanese forces at Kokumbona in the Matanikau area. A gap existed by way of a swampy creek in the southern side of the American lines. Between November 9 and 11, Shoji and between 2,000 and 3,000 of his men escaped into the jungle to the south. On November 12, the Americans completely overran and killed all the remaining Japanese soldiers left in the pocket. The Americans counted the bodies of 450-475 Japanese dead in the Koli Point area and captured most of Shoji's heavy weapons and provisions. The American forces suffered 40 killed and 120 wounded in the operation.

On November 5, Vandegrift ordered Carlson to take his raiders, march overland from Aola, and attack any of Shoji's forces that had escaped from Koli Point. With the rest of the companies from his battalion, which arrived a few days alter, Carlson and his troops set off on a 29-day patrol from Aola to the Lunga perimeter. During the patrol, the raiders fought several battles with Shoji's retreating forces, killing almost 500 of them, while suffering 16 killed themselves. In addition to the losses sustained from attacks by Carlson's raiders, tropical diseases and a lack of food felled many more of Shoji's men. By the time Shoji's forces reached the Lunga River in mid-November, about halfway to the Matanikau, only 1,300 men remained with the main body. When Shoji reached the 17th Army positions west of the Matanikau, only 700 to 800 survivors were still with him. Most of the survivors from Shoji's force joined other Japanese units defending the Mount Austen and upper Matanikau River area.

The Americans and Japanese remained facing each other along a line just west of Point Cruz for the next six weeks.

Naval Battle of Guadalcanal

In early November 1942, allied intelligence learned that the Japanese were preparing again to try to retake Henderson Field. Therefore, the U. S. sent Task Force 67, a large reinforcement and resupply convoy carrying Marine replacements, two U. S. Army infantry battalions, and ammunition and food, commanded by Turner, to Guadalcanal on November 11. The merchant supply ships were protected by two task groups, commanded by Rear Admirals *Daniel J. Callaghan* and *Norman Scott*, and aircraft from Henderson Field. The ships were attacked several times on November 11 and 12 by Japanese aircraft from Rabaul staging through an air base at Buin, Bougainville, but most were unloaded without serious damage.

U.S. reconnaissance aircraft spotted the approach of Vice Admiral Hiroaki Abe's bombardment force and passed a warning to the Allied command.

Around 01:30 on November 13, Callaghan's force intercepted Abe's bombardment group between Guadalcanal and Savo Island. In addition to the two battleships, Abe's force included one light cruiser and 11 destroyers. In the pitch darkness, two warship forces intermingled before opening fire at unusually close quarters. In the resulting melee, Abe's warships sank or severely damaged all but one cruiser and one destroyer in Callaghan's force and both Callaghan and Scott were killed. In spite of his defeat of Callaghan's force, Abe ordered his warships to retire without bombarding Henderson Field.

Around 02:00 on November 14, a cruiser and destroyer under Gunichi Mikawa from Rabaul conducted an unopposed bombardment of Henderson Field. The bombardment caused some damage but failed to put the airfield or most of its aircraft out of operation.

On November 26, Japanese Lieutenant General Hitoshi Imamura took command of the newly formed Eighth Area Army at Rabaul. The new command encompassed both Hyakutake's 17th Army and the 18th Army in New Guinea. One of Imamura's first priorities upon assuming command was the continuation of the attempts to retake Henderson Field and Guadalcanal. The Allied offensive at Buna in New Guinea, however, changed Imamura's priorities. Because the Allied attempt to take Buna was considered a more severe threat at Rabaul, Imamura postponed further major reinforcement efforts to Guadalcanal to concentrate on the situation in New Guinea.

Battle of Tassafaronga

The Japanese continued to experience problems in delivering sufficient supplies to sustain their troops on Guadalcanal. Attempts to use only submarines the last two weeks in November failed to provide sufficient food for Hyakutake's forces. A separate attempt to establish bases in the central Solomons to facilitate barge convoys to Guadalcanal also failed because of destructive Allied air attacks. On November 26, the 17th Army notified Imamura that it faced a critical food crisis. Some front-line units had not been re-supplied for six days and even the rear-area troops were on one-third rations. The situation forced the Japanese to return to using destroyers to deliver the necessary supplies.

Eighth Fleet personnel devised a plan to help reduce the exposure of destroyers delivering supplies to Guadalcanal. Large oil or gas drums were cleaned and filled with medical supplies and food, with enough air space to provide buoyancy, and strung together with rope. When the destroyers arrived at Guadalcanal they would make a sharp turn, and the drums would be cut loose and a swimmer or boat from shore could pick up the buoyed end of a rope and return it to the beach where the soldiers could haul in the supplies.

The Eighth Fleet's Guadalcanal Reinforcement Unit (The Tokyo Express), currently commanded by Raizo Tanaka, was tasked by Mikawa with making the first of five scheduled runs to Tassafaronga on Guadalcanal using the drum method on the night of November 30. Notified by intelligence sources of the Japanese supply attempt, Halsey ordered the newly formed Task Force 67, under the command of U. S. Rear Admiral Carleton H. Wright, to intercept Tanaka's force off Guadalcanal.

At 22:40 on November 30, Tanaka's force arrived off Guadalcanal and prepared to unload the supply barrels. Meanwhile, Wright's warships were approaching through Ironbottom Sound from the opposite direction. Wright's destroyers detected Tanaka's force on radar and the destroyer commander requested permission to attack with torpedoes. Wright waited four minutes before giving permission, allowing Tanaka's force to escape from an optimum firing setup. All of the American torpedoes missed their targets. At the same time, Wright's cruisers opened fire, quickly hitting and destroying one of the Japanese guard destroyers. The rest of Tanaka's warships abandoned the supply mission, increased speed, turned, and launched a total of 44 torpedoes in the direction of Wright's cruisers.

The Japanese torpedoes hit and sank the U. S. Cruiser *Northampton* and heavily damaged the cruisers *Minneapolis, New Orleans*, and *Pensacola*. The rest of Tanaka's destroyers escaped without damage, but failed to deliver any of the provisions to Guadalcanal.

Japanese Decision to Withdraw

On December 12, the Japanese Navy proposed that Guadalcanal be abandoned. At the same time, several army staff officers at the Imperial General Headquarters (IGH) also suggested that further efforts to retake Guadalcanal would be impossible. A delegation, led by IJA Colonel Joichiro Sanada, chief of the IGH's operations section, visited Rabaul on December 19 and consulted Imamura and his staff. Upon the delegation's return to Tokyo, Sanada recommended that Guadalcanal be abandoned. The IGH's top leaders agreed with Sanada's recommendation on December 26 and ordered their staffs to begin drafting plans for a withdrawal from Guadalcanal, establishment of a new defense line in the central Solomons, and a shifting of priorities and resources to the campaign in New Guinea.

Aftermath

After Guadalcanal the Japanese were clearly on the defensive in the Pacific. The constant pressure to reinforce Guadalcanal had weakened Japanese efforts in other theaters, contributing to a successful Australian and American counteroffensive in New Guinea which culminated in the capture of the key bases of Buna and Gona in early 1943. The Allies had gained a strategic initiative which they never relinquished. In June, the Allies launched Operation Cartwheel, which, after modification in August 1943, formalized the strategy of isolating Rabaul and cutting its sea lines of communication. The subsequent successful neutralization of Rabaul and the forces centered there facilitated the South West Pacific campaign under General *Douglas MacArthur* and the Central Pacific island-hopping campaign under Admiral *Chester Nimitz*, with both efforts successfully advancing toward Japan. The remaining Japanese defenses in the South Pacific area were then either destroyed or bypassed by Allied forces as the war progressed to its ultimate conclusion.

Significance

The U. S. Navy and Merchant Marine suffered such high personnel losses during the campaign that it refused to publicly release total casualty figures for years. However, as the campaign continued, and the American public became more and more aware of the plight and perceived heroism of the American forces on Guadalcanal, more forces were dispatched to the area. This spelled trouble for Japan as its military-industrial complex was unable to match the output of American industry and manpower. Thus, as the campaign wore on the Japanese were losing irreplaceable units while the Americans were rapidly replacing and even augmenting their forces.

The Guadalcanal campaign was costly to Japan strategically and in material losses and manpower. Roughly 25,000 experienced ground troops were killed during the campaign. The drain on resources directly contributed to Japan's failure to achieve its objectives in the New Guinea campaign. Japan also lost control of the southern Solomons and the ability to interdict Allied shipping to Australia. Japan's major base at Rabaul was now further directly threatened by Allied air power. Most important, scarce Japanese land, air, and naval forces had disappeared forever into the Guadalcanal jungle and surrounding sea. The Japanese could not replace the aircraft and ships destroyed and sunk in this campaign, as well as their highly trained and veteran crews, especially the naval aircrews, nearly as quickly as the Allies.

After the victory at the Battle of Midway, America was able to establish naval parity in the Pacific. However, this fact alone did not change the direction of the war. It was only after the Allied victories in Guadalcanal and New Guinea that the Japanese offensive thrust was ended and the strategic initiative passed to the Allies, as it proved, permanently. The Guadalcanal Campaign ended all Japanese expansion attempts and placed the Allies in a position of clear supremacy. It thus can be argued that this Allied victory was the first step in a long string of successes that eventually led to the surrender of Japan and the occupation of the Japanese home islands.

The "Europe first" policy of the United States had initially only allowed for defensive actions against Japanese expansion, in order to focus resources on defeating Germany. However, Admiral King's argument for the Guadalcanal invasion, as well as its successful implementation, convinced President Franklin D. Roosevelt that the Pacific Theater could be pursued offensively as well. By the end of 1942, it was clear that Japan had lost the Guadalcanal campaign, a serious blow to Japan's strategic plans for defense of their empire and an unanticipated defeat at the hands of the Americans.

Dangerous Convoys

World War II saw the continued use of convoys to protect the huge logistic sealift originating from the United States which had become Roosevelt's "Arsenal of Democracy." Although convoy operations were slow to be implemented along our east coast, they were used throughout the war for virtually all cargo ships transiting the Atlantic. The S.S. **JOHN W. BROWN** sailed in a convoy for her wartime voyages across the Atlantic and in the Mediterranean Sea. Only the faster ships, including passenger liners converted to troop transports, sailed independently. Although convoy escort forces were relatively weak at the beginning of the war, they would soon improve dramatically both in terms of numbers and capability. By 1943, improved sensors and weapons were installed on escort vessels and aircraft became available to augment the surface escort forces.

A Large Convoy
Merchant ships being escorted by a land-based patrol plane

Sailing in a convoy did not guarantee safe passage. While convoys did offer protection for merchant ships, once the convoy was detected, additional U-boats and aircraft could be directed to the location which, for them, was a target-rich environment. As the capability of the escort forces improved, the shoe was shifted to the other foot. Enemy submarines drawn to the vicinity of a convoy concentrated them in an area where they were more easily detected and attacked by the convoy escorts.

Two wartime convoys stand out as major battles that resulted in the significant loss of Allied merchant ships. Both occurred in the summer of 1942 with Convoy PQ-17 sailing to Murmansk in July and the Operation Pedestal convoy sailing to Malta the following month. About two-thirds of the merchant ships in every convoy were lost to enemy action and the latter operation saw major losses to the escort force as well.

The Run to Murmansk

The run to Murmansk was dreaded by most seamen. The weather in the Barents Sea was horrible, particularly in the winter. In summer months, there was near continuous daylight when sailing north of the Arctic Circle, making convoy detection and tracking easier for the enemy. German submarines, aircraft, and capital ships were based in occupied northern Norway close to the convoy routes. The distance from the coast that convoys could sail to minimize that threat was limited by the edge of the Arctic ice pack. During the course of the war, forty-two convoys with a total of 848 ships made the run to Murmansk. Sixty-five ships were lost, half of them from Convoy PQ-17. Despite the hazards faced on this route, Arctic convoys were continued for both political and strategic reasons. Until the Normandy invasion in 1944, the Russian forces were the primary focus of the German army in Europe and it was important to keep them supplied and in the battle.

The heavy losses suffered by PQ-17 made it the most ill-fated convoy to Murmansk. In a still controversial decision, the Royal Navy, fearing the sortie of the German battleship TIRPITZ and other surface forces to attack the convoy, ordered the escort withdrawn and the American merchant ships to scatter and proceed independently. The now unprotected ships were easy prey for German submarines and aircraft.

The Russian Gauntlet

That night, as the merchant ships fanned out in several directions, their uneasy crews did not sleep well. They wore their clothes, boots, and life jackets to bed.

On June 27, 1942, Convoy PQ-17 sailed from Rejkevik, Iceland, with thirty-four merchant vessels, including six new Liberty ships loaded with military supplies and equipment, five previous convoys had been attacked and ships were sunk, so security was especially heavy this time around. The original convoy was protected by an English escort of four cruisers, two antiaircraft cruisers, nine destroyers, and two submarines, along with other vessels. In addition, one aircraft carrier, two battleships, three additional cruisers, and eight destroyers were nearby, in the North Sea.

The following Wednesday, July 1, German torpedo bombers began attacking the convoy. One of the merchant seamen who survived the PQ-17 debacle was Frank Medeiros of the SS *Gateway City*. His ship was an old World War One "Hog Islander" – named for the place it had been built, on the Delaware River. The smokestack of the *Gateway City* always belched black smoke.

The losses to Convoy PQ-17 were catastrophic indeed. Twenty-three of the thirty-four merchant ships in the convoy were sunk between July 4 and July 10, with a loss of more than one hundred thousand tons of cargo. This included 3,350 motor vehicles, 430 tanks, and 210 military aircraft – all desperately needed by the Soviet Union to fight off the invading German Army. Included were four Liberty ships on their maiden voyage.

When only a small percentage of Convoy PQ-17 made it to port, Russian authorities initially thought the Americans and British were lying to them, that they had not sent the promised supplies and equipment. But as evidence accumulated, the Soviets soon learned what had really happened.

David Milton, a merchant seaman who survived the Murmansk Run, described how desperate the Russians were for military equipment and supplies: "We finally got to Murmansk with these huge locomotives on the very top of the deck. The Russians unloaded them right onto the tracks. They brought up freight cars and attached them to the locomotives. We unloaded the tanks right onto these flatcars. They'd right away fire up the locomotives and shoot right out to the war front. I mean, they weren't playing around."

Convoy PQ-17, designated by the British Admiralty in charge, still stands as the biggest disaster of all. *Winston Churchill* referred to it as "one of the most melancholy episodes in the whole of the war." It came to be known as "the Hell Convoy." More American merchant mariners were casualties of the Murmansk Run than on any other convoy in WW II.

One survivor said that many of the men had gangrene in their fingers and toes, and recounted the horrors of the hospital. "Unless you have personally smelled flesh rotting with gangrene, you could not imagine the stench."

Murmansk Run
by John Albert

> *I signed on the SS Wind Rush in April of 1942 and arrived in Loch Ewue, Scotland a few weeks later. For some reason, we stayed in the British Isles for six months in various places such as the Firth of Clyde. We went to Ireland for bottom inspection. Then we went*

to London where all the cargo was unloaded and put in warehouses. Next we went into dry-dock. After dry-docking, the cargo was reloaded. We found out later that a decision had been made to hold up convoys to Murmansk until the winter months because the last convoy (PQ-17) had lost so many ships that it was deemed advisable to wait for the winter months when the hours of darkness were extremely long and German aircraft would have fewer hours of daylight to find a convoy.

In December 1942, we sailed in a convoy from the Thames for Murmansk. We arrived in Murmansk on Christmas morning of 1942. On our way to Murmansk, a German cruiser came out of Norway and fired on our convoy. We could see the flash of her guns but she did not have the range and her shells overshot the convoy. Our escorts returned her fire and chased her back to Norway although they did not actually follow her to Norway since they did not want to leave our convoy unprotected. Before departing, she actually sank one of our destroyers and damaged another. We were supposed to be the first convoy to arrive in Murmansk without the loss of a ship. According to German radio propaganda, Hitler promised us this wouldn't be the case on our return trip.

While in Murmansk, every hour or hour and a half we would get an air raid. I've been told that the German airfields were only about sixty miles away. There were dog fights between German planes and Russian fighters. The bombs were mostly of the incendiary type. We had two airplanes on deck and bombs in the number 2 hatch. When they were unloaded and assembled, the Russians made a bombing run on the German airbase in Finland and this stopped the bombing of Murmansk for about a week. Our merchant ship gun crews had been shooting at anything coming over. In some instances, we may have shot up Russian planes as the Russians came out with a new order that when an air attack was imminent, a Russian plane would *lay down a strip of smoke in the sky. Anything on the merchant ship side of the smoke screen was a legitimate target for the merchant ship gunners, but shots were not to be fired on the other side of the screen as Russian fighters would be fighting with the Germans on the other side of the screen.*

We were able to have shore liberty, but there was not much to do. The Germans bombed the only bar in town. Prior to that bombing, we could get one ration of vodka a day. But there was nothing else to see or do.

The stevedores and longshoremen were all women and they drove the deck engineer crazy with the way they handled the winches while discharging cargo. They also drove the deck gang crazy. They were getting backlashes on the drums of the winches. The deck gang was kept busy just keeping the cargo handling gear in operating order. The women longshoremen seemed friendly enough, perhaps wanting us to give them food. However, the Russian men showed a strong hostility toward Americans. We finally finished discharging cargo and moved out into the anchorage to await the forming of a return convoy. At last on the 29th of January, we got underway for our return back to our world. Hitler kept his promise. Our convoy came under heavy attack and before we reached the haven of Scotland we had lost 16 ships. We sailed in a large convoy returning to the U.S., but out in the mid North Atlantic we came under a relentless attack again. For five days and nights we were under attack from the submarine wolf packs. The nights were the worst. These subs would slip into the convoy on the surface. We actually heard the sound of diesels of a sub as it slipped into the convoy between our bow and the stern of the ship in front of us, but the bow lookouts could not see a thing. Only the sound of diesels gave us a warning and flares were shot up. We were having two or three ships a night torpedoed. There had been a Norwegian ship in *our column directly in front of us. The Norwegian Captain started his own zigzagging in the convoy, and this made it very difficult for our lockouts to see his very dim stern marker light. Our Captain got permission from the convoy commander to swap positions with the Norwegian ship, and that same night the Norwegian ship got torpedoed. If we had not swapped positions, it would have been us instead.*

These wolf pack attacks tapered off after our convoy got into range of long distance air cover. Before we went back, we ran into a bad storm which caused a rupture in our fuel tanks which let salt water into our fuel. We had to drop back to the rear of the convoy while our engineers worked frantically to drain water from the lower suction of the settling tanks. Then we would be able to steam ahead and get back into position before water hit the fires in the boilers again. We and two other ships were allowed to go into Halifax, Nova Scotia for repairs while the rest of the convoy steamed on to New York. The SS Wind Rush was a good ship but she was an old one having been built during WWI. She was a flush deck ship. Prior to the war, she had been used in the timber trade on the West coast. After repairs and bunkering, we made it back to the Big Apple and paid off in New York.

Only those who have sailed in convoys know how the metal walls of the hull move in and out when depth charges go off. Someone likened this hull movement to the leather skin of a bass drum when it is pounded by the drummer. I do not recommend Murmansk for a winter vacation. It is colder than "blue cold" up there. Some of my shipmates said they would prefer the fires of Hell to another trip to Murmansk in the winter.

God bless all those shipmates, be they American or Allied, who sailed not for money but for their patriotic duty and doing their part to overcome the tyranny of Hitler.

Operation Pedestal and SS Ohio Save Malta with the Help of Two American Merchant Mariners

In mid-1942, the war was going badly for the Allies. During the first six months U-boats sank 3,250,000 tons of shipping in the Atlantic (an average freighter was 7,000 tons). Rommel rolled through Northern Africa, threatening the Suez Canal, but stopped 35 miles short of Alexandria, Egypt, because of a shortage of supplies. The Nazi war machine reached Stalingrad, with plans to head through the Caucasus for the Middle East oil fields. The Allies had Gibraltar, Malta, and Egypt. The Axis controlled France, Italy, Yugoslavia, Greece, and most of northern Africa. A few countries were neutral (Turkey) or pro-Axis (Spain).

There was an invalidated story that a French pilot was flying a German plane near the coast of occupied France who had orders not to report anything back by radio. He saw the Operation Pedestal Convoy and inadvertently forgot his orders and made his report. The Germans heard and knew they had to immediately respond to this Convoy headed for Malta. It was a top secret, but was too big to hide sometimes stretching 10 miles at sea.

Adolph Hitler planned an invasion of Malta with Admiral Raeder, commander-in-chief of the German Navy. But at the last minute, he canceled it. "I am a coward at sea," he said. "It was the greatest mistake of the Axis in the whole war in this theater," said Admiral Weichold, the German commander in the Mediterranean.

The SS *Ohio* steamed from Texas to Glasgow, where she was turned over to a British crew, and a new master, *Dudley Mason*, was assigned.

With Malta facing capitulation to the Axis, Prime Minister Churchill met with FDR and borrowed the SS *Ohio*. The Texas Company ship was the biggest and fastest tanker in the world. She was Malta's last hope, because there was no survival without the 107,000 barrels of oil carried in her thirty-three honeycombed tanks for antiaircraft generators on Malta and the Royal Navy submarines hunting Rommel's supply ships.

Another very dangerous convoy run was the one to Malta. The island of Malta was a very important strategic British base in the Mediterranean. Located in a position to control the narrow sea between Sicily and Cape Bon on the African coast, this isolated island outpost helped maintain the Royal Navy presence in the Mediterranean and restricted the Axis' ability to resupply Rommel's forces fighting in North Africa. The island was subject to regular aerial attack by the enemy in an attempt to neutralize or capture it. Sending convoys to Malta from either of the British bases at Gibraltar and Alexandria, Egypt was extremely hazardous due to the threat of enemy air and naval forces based in Italy and Sicily. Thirty merchant ships had already been lost in the effort to resupply Malta. However, a viable British presence there was a critical aspect of the war in the Mediterranean and Malta had to be maintained despite the cost.

In the month following the PQ-17 convoy, the British formed a convoy to sail from England via Gibraltar to replenish Malta named Operation Pedestal. Supplies of fuel and food were nearly exhausted and the resupply effort has to get through. The convoy of 14 relatively fast merchant ships was formed in August 1942 and protected by a formidable naval escort. It was probably the most heavily defended convoy of the war for the number of ships involved. Three American vessels were included in the convoy. The tanker SS *OHIO* was reflagged and sailed with a British Merchant Navy master and crew. The SANTA ELISA and ALMERIA LYKES were in the convoy with American crews; both ships would be lost. (There were no Liberty ships in Operation Pedestal. They were too slow.)

Great Britain had no tankers capable of 16 knots, so President Franklin Delano Roosevelt lent the SS *Ohio* to Winston Churchill for use in supplying Malta.

The tanker SS *Ohio* was launched on April 20, 1940 at Sun Shipbuilding Yard in Chester, Pennsylvania for Texas Oil Company. In anticipation of war and due to unofficial conversations between the American military and the oil company, the SS *Ohio* was the largest tanker built at that time. At 9,263 tons 485 feet long, she and her sister ships held 170,000 barrels of oil. With 9,000 shaft horsepower Westinghouse turbine engines, they were rated at 16 knots, but in sea trials *SS Ohio* made 19 knots.

Time lines of passage through the Mediterranean:

August 10-11 Night: American merchant ships Almeria Lykes (C3) and Santa Elisa (C20) entered Gibralter in heavy fog. "Get through at all costs" were the orders.

August 12: SS Ohio's tanker torpedoed by Italian submarine and on fire. Manages 13 knots after repair. 20 Junkers 88s attack. US Gunners on the Almeria Lykes shoot down two planes.

August 13: Santa Elisa (US) hit by torpedo, entire ship on fire and abandoned after Larsen and chief mate fought the fire over four hours.
Almeria Lykes (US) torpedoed. Sinks immediately.,
Junkers 88 crashes onto Ohio. Ohio avoids mines, torpedoes and circling torpedoes. Two bombs straddle her; lift her out of the water. Boilers are blown and she is dead in the water at 10:50 A.M.
Junkers 88 attacks on Ohio, nearly split her in two as a bomb hits the same area as a torpedo. British crew abandons ship.

August 14: <above> **Frederick Larsen, Jr.**, Third Mate and **Francis Dales**, Cadet-Midshipman from the U.S. Merchant Marine Academy, crew members of the Santa Elisa volunteer to man the guns on the SS *Ohio* during tow. The rescue destroyer and another destroyer steamed in, lashed themselves on either side of the stricken tanker, and dragged her along in a determined attempt to get her to the port. The tankers decks and superstructures had been almost completely wrecked by the incessant bombardment.

Larsen boarded the SS *Ohio* in the middle of the night. Joined by Dales, they repaired the 40-millimeter Bofors single-barrel antiaircraft gun on the stern. Larsen's anxiety to get into the fight caused him to take inventory of her armament. He found an antiaircraft gun mounted abaft the stack which needed only minor repairs to put it in action. The young cadet of his own ship, Francis A. Dales, a British Gunner's mate, and three of his men volunteered to help him. Though the ships were then constantly under attack, they boarded her, repaired the gun and manned it, with Larsen taking the trainer's position, and the gunner's mate and the cadet alternating as pointers. The shackled ships, inching along and making perfect targets, were assailed by concentrated enemy air power.

That entire day wave after wave of German and Italian bombers dived at them and were beaten off by a heavy barrage. Bombs straddled them, scoring near misses, but no direct hits were made until noon the next day, when the tanker finally received a bomb down her stack which blew out the bottom of her engine room. Though she continued to settle until her decks were awash, they fought her through until dusk that day brought them under the protection of the hard fighting air force of Malta.

The magnificent courage of this young third officer and cadet-midshipman constitutes a degree of heroism which will be an enduring inspiration to seamen of the United States Merchant Marine everywhere.

August 15: Ohio arrives at Grand Harbour at 9:30 A.M. to cheering crowds.
October 20, 1942:

**The President of the United States takes
great pleasure in presenting the
Merchant Marine Distinguished Service Medal to
Frederick August Larsen, Jr., Junior Third Officer
and
Francis A. Dales, Cadet-Midshipman
U.S. Merchant Marine Academy
For Heroism Beyond the Call of Duty**

A crippled ship and two American merchant mariners turned the tide of World War II. "In Valletta Harbor, we were saluted like a victorious Navy ship," said Larsen. "Crowds of people were singin' and shoutin' and screamin' and playin' bands and it was quite a thrill comin' in. I was sittin' up on top of the Borfors with some of the volunteers."

"They were playing *The star-spangled Banner* for us," said Dales.

With the delivery of the *Ohio's* oil to Malta, the 10th Submarine Flotilla had diesel fuel again, and was able to resume its attacks on Axis convoys supplying Rommel in north Africa. The Royal Malta Artillery had kerosene for the generators that powered the pumps and lights.

Thousands and thousands of people in Malta faced starvation according to reports from the island of Malta, and many did starve to death.

The Voyage of the SS James Eagan Layne and Purvis Evans

The SS James Eagan Layne was a munitions ship that died like a great beached whale. Fortunately, her crew was lucky souls who returned home with hardly a scratch. Two days old, the Layne embarked from New Orleans just before Christmas 1944 and put in at San Jacinto Ordnance Depot in Texas for a cargo of bombs. She then sailed to New York and joined a convoy bound for England. Her crew consisted of 42 seamen and 27 Naval Armed Guard. Her Master was William Sleek.

Without incident, the Layne's bombs were unloaded in England. She then sailed uneventfully around to Barry, Wales for a cargo of Army material intended for Ghent, Belgium.

On March 21, 1945, about 12 miles off Plymouth, England, the convoy was formed up into two columns. The Layne was Vice Commodore and leader of the second column when a torpedo struck between #four and #five holds on the starboard side. The explosion blew off #five hatch covers and caused a crack in the hull on the port side from the water line to the bulwarks at

#four hatch. The shaft alley was flooded and the shaft broken. The engine was immediately shut down, the steering gear was put out of order, #four and #five holds were flooded and the bulkhead went down by the stern until water was flush with the deck of the after gun tub. The ship was abandoned on Captain's orders about ten minutes after the attack in four lifeboats and one life raft. Some of the crew was picked up by the British SS Monkstone and landed in Southampton. The remainder of the ship's crew was taken aboard the HMS Flaunt. The Master, Engineers and a seaman reboarded the ship and remained until she was beached. HMS Flaunt towed the Layne to Whitesand Bay, England for beaching. She was declared a total loss. At high water, only the stack and top of the mast could be seen.

The ship was named in honor of the 2nd Engineer lost in the first torpedoing of the SS ESSO Baton Rouge on April 8, 1942 about 13 miles off Brunswick, GA. The ESSO Baton Rouge, which was sunk by Reinhard Hardegen's U-123, was re-floated and repaired; then about 400 miles south of the Azores, the ship was torpedoed again on February 23, 1943.

The Layne's attacker, U-1195, was sunk in the English Channel by HMS Watchman on April 6, 1945.

Like many who became merchant seamen during WW II, Purvis Evans was too young for the draft. His parents wouldn't sign for his Navy enlistment papers, so he worked as a welder at the Wainwright shipyard in Panama City, FL. He decided to sail on Liberty ships such as the ones he helped build and enrolled in the U. S. Maritime Service and trained at the U.S.M.S. Training School at St. Petersburg, FL. After some training he was shipped out and was assigned duty as a Wiper on the SS ESSO Layne. The ship was just two days old when she steamed down the Mississippi from New Orleans.

Every seaman who was ever torpedoed remembers where he was in the ship and what he was doing at the time the torpedo struck. Purvis said,

"It was the loudest explosion I've ever heard. Years later I witnessed an artillery barrage demo at Ft. Benning, and the noise did not compare with the torpedo explosion. When the torpedo struck, the ship shuddered as if hit broadside by a giant wave. My first thought was that the Navy Armed Guard had a terrible accident and wrecked the Layne. Alarms and telegraph bells immediately sounded, and the engine was stopped. The fireman pulled the lever on the Fuel Oil cutoff valve stopping fuel to the burners. The engine room's four-man crew rushed for our lifeboat stations. A corvette was sowing depth charges a few hundred feet to the starboard, so we knew what had happened. A light smoke drifted from the burst hatches, their canvas and wooden covers gone. The safety valves from the boilers went off once (cherry red firebrick in a boiler's furnace still generate steam even with the fires out). The popping safety valves did not help our nerves. Though the stern was down in the sea past gunwale, the ship no longer seemed to be sinking. A raft launched astern splashed into the water, and a few of us boarded it. Within minutes, a British merchant vessel rescued us from the raft, and a Royal Navy ship picked up the rest of the crew from the four lifeboats.

The only injury reported was a cut lip when a Navy Armed Guard sailor was tossed from his cot by the explosion. We were given clothes and shoes by the Red Cross and Salvation Army and then sent by train to London. I was wearing an Italian POW jacket. The city suffered V-2 buzz-bomb attacks nightly. One of our crew went with a lady to visit a museum, and when they returned to her flat, they found a block wide hole filled with rubble where her flat had been. The Layne's crew's good luck was still holding. Saddened by losing our great 92-day-old ship, we were repatriated to New York aboard the troopship SS Brazil."

The SS James Eagan Layne was built by the Delta Shipbuilding Corporation, New Orleans, Louisiana in 1944 and was operated by the US Navigation Company of New York.

Seafarers' Tales

The Real Story of D-day
New York Times, June 9, 1944

LONDON – D-day would not have been possible without the Merchant Marine. Now that the long-awaited day is history and great Allied forces have been landed in France, it is permitted to indicate the part played by these intrepid civilians, whose deeds for the most part have gone unsung. It is not generally realized that the Merchant Marine has the largest ratio of casualties of any branch of the services, and many of the names on the list are not classified "wounded" or "missing." They were those of the men whose grave is the sea. Working side-by-side with the British Merchant Navy and the Allied fleets, the American Merchant Marine has reached a new peak of glory, and into this latest venture it has brought all the hard-earned experience of such historic episodes as the African landings and the bitterly-fought Arctic runs to Russia. For weeks before D-day hundreds of merchant ships which had been diverted from their regular runs for the invasion service roamed the waters near the British Isles without a port to come to. They were kept outside so the enemy would not see any great ship concentration at any principal port. At the prearranged time they rendezvoused, picked up their priceless cargo and sailed for France. Undaunted by the threat of air attacks, sea mines, surface fire, submarines or coastal batteries they fulfilled their mission according to schedule and returned to Britain's shores to start a shuttle service that will not end before Germany's unconditional surrender. At their sides are a thousand or more British merchant ships with 50,000 seamen, many of whom have old scores to settle –scores that started at Dunkerque and were aggravated at Crete. The ships that went to France were of every conceivable type of transport. Some were former luxury liners that even confirmed round-the-world travelers would no longer recognize. Others were no larger than good-sized barges or sea-going tugs. But most were new, the internationally-known Liberty ships, designed to meet the needs of war.

One way to understand the Second World War is to appreciate the critical role of merchant shipping . . . the availability or non-availability of merchant shipping determined what the Allies could or could not do militarily . . . when sinkings of Allied merchant vessels exceeded production, when slow turnarounds, convoy delays, roundabout routing, and long voyages taxed transport severely, or when the cross-Channel invasion planned for 1942 had to be postponed for many months for reasons which included insufficient shipping. Had these ships not been produced, the war would have been in all likelihood prolonged many months, if not years. Some argue the Allies would have lost as there would not have existed the means to carry the personnel, supplies, and equipment needed by the combined Allies to defeat the Axis powers. (It took seven to 15 tons of supplies to support one soldier for one year.) The U.S. wartime merchant fleet . . . constituted one of the most significant contributions made by any nation to the eventual winning of the Second World War . . . In the final assessment; the huge US merchant fleet . . . provided critical logistical support to the war effort.

Merchant Marine Still Seeking Respect
'They couldn't have won the war without us'

by Mark Brown, Sun-Times Columnist, May 27, 2007

When the United States entered World War II, *Frank Dorner* tried to join the Marine Corps, but he flunked the physical. A problem with his teeth, they told him.

That's when he saw a recruiting poster in his Southwest Side neighborhood that beckoned: "Join the Merchant Marine. Be a Hero. Help Your Country."

Dorner didn't even know what the Merchant Marine was when he went to the recruiting office, but they didn't mind his teeth. Days later, he was on his way to Sheepshead Bay, NY, for training.

'I know I helped our country.'

For the next three years, Dorner sailed the seas in support of the U.S. war effort. His career as a mariner was finally curtailed after two torpedoes from a German sub slammed into the hull of the SS Henry Miller off the coast of Morocco in January 1945. While the captain ordered the sailors to abandon ship, Dorner was part of a skeleton crew that stayed aboard and nursed it back to port.

All these years later, though, Dorner and his fellow members of the Merchant Marine still hunger for the respect they feel was denied them when they got home. Because they were technically civilians and not members of the military, they not only weren't treated as heroes, they weren't even considered veterans.

"I loved what I did, and I know I helped our country," Dorner, 86, said from his kitchen table at the start of another Memorial Day weekend during which members of the Merchant Marine will have to elbow their way to the podium at veteran recognition ceremonies to remind the speakers that they were "over there," too.

Dorner and the other merchant seamen sailed the cargo ships that delivered the weapons, ammunition, food, fuel and other supplies to the U.S. military and its allies. That made them a target every time they left home port.

Recruiting Poster

These posters were used by the War Shipping Administration
during the war years to recruit merchant seaman.

"They couldn't have won the war without us."

This is a refrain so common among the WW II merchant seamen that it became the title of a book on their experiences written by Pete Peterson, a former WW II mariner who worked many years with a Chicago ad agency.

But the mariners had no uniforms – unless you count blue jeans and a T-shirt– and were similarly lacking military discipline. Employed by shipping companies, they found their ships through labor unions – all of which made them the object of mistrust by the real military.

Some called them draft dodgers, but if they were trying to stay out of harm's way, the merchant seamen made a very poor choice.

By the reckoning of their own historians, the Merchant Marine casualty rate during WW II was exceeded only by the Marine Corps, with 9,500 deaths out of the 243,000 who served.

They died "from torpedoes, aerial bombs, collisions, shell bursts and machine-gun bullets, frigid seas, flames, exploding cargoes. From drowning trapped below decks or from freezing or starving adrift in oar-less lifeboats."

So wrote Bruce Felknor, an Evanston retiree who authored The U.S. Merchant Marine at War, 1775-1945.

Felknor, who was 4F in the draft during WW II because of respiratory problems before being taken as a radio officer in the Merchant Marine, went on to become an executive editor at Encyclopaedia Britannica after the war.

"They used to say the Merchant Marine didn't care what your health was as long as you could climb a gangway," said Felknor, 85, his voice a barely audible whisper these days, the breathing problems having progressed into chronic obstructive pulmonary disease while cancer surgery damaged a vocal cord.

Time is running out for all of them now, of course, as it is for all WW II veterans. We figure barely 2-3,000 WW II merchant seamen survive.

Pushing Bill to Get Pension

That's why they're making a big push for legislation already proposed in Congress to pay the survivors a small monthly pension. They say they want it for the belated recognition, although many of them could use the cash, too.

The merchant seamen often cite a quotation from President Franklin Roosevelt when he signed the GI Bill in 1944.

"I trust Congress will soon provide similar opportunities to members of the Merchant Marines who have risked their lives time and time again during war for the welfare of their country," Roosevelt said. But he died, and Congress never did.

A court decision enabled them to qualify for veterans' status in 1988, making them eligible for medical care and burial in our national cemeteries. But the merchant seamen still feel shortchanged.

They helped our country. Many were heroes.

A Great Event But a Snub to the Merchant Marine
by Bob Ulrich, President, Sacramento Valley Chapter, AMMV

> *It was a beautifully orchestrated event. A thin line of cars threaded its way down the two-lane country road leading to the soon to be dedicated Sacramento Valley VA National Cemetery. Police and*

Highway Patrol officers directed traffic to an area set up to park the multitude of cars transporting the hundreds who were arriving for the event. Plenty of busses were available to shuttle people to the nearby cemetery and the event was beautiful: a flyover of planes presumably from Travis, the Air Force Band, speakers on the platform representing Congress, the VA, California and others. There were hundreds of American flags. In front of the speakers' stand were the flags of the military branches who were being honored (no Merchant Marine flag here). The band played the anthems of the various branches and veterans who had served in those branches were asked to stand. Those of us there, with our Merchant Marine hats and ribbons, waited without too much hope. Finally the band played the Air Force song and as the band members stood, to be honored themselves, we knew it was all over. We could wait till hell freezes over but we would not hear the Merchant Marine song. Again, it seems we will be accepted for burial, but we would not be acknowledged and we would not be honored. We were insulted by the omission. Alert!! At least six new National VA Cemeteries are to be dedicated soon. Pressure your local authorities. It didn't work here but it may yet result in change as they are aware of our feelings and seem to be seeking authority or precedence. I have given them our music by the Kings Point Regimental Band. Help us all by keeping the pressure on in your area as these cemeteries are being dedicated.

The Merchant Mariners of World War II Need Some Recognition
by Mark Schwed, Palm Beach Post Staff Writer, Tuesday, May 22, 2007

Nearly 65 years have passed, yet Calvin G. Berry still hears them screaming. He is 83 now, retired, living in peace in Cape Coral. But when the screams come, he is young again – 19 years old – covered in oil, floating in the chilly Pacific Ocean, watching his ship, the SS Larry Doheny, sink from a Japanese torpedo fired just off the California coast during World War II.

Seventy feet away, trapped in the burning fuel surrounding the sinking oil tanker, are two of his shipmates. They scream for help, but all he can do is watch them burn to death.

"It's horrible," he says, choking back tears as the images and sounds of that foggy October night flood his mind. "A lot of time has passed, but it just doesn't get any better. You try to block it out. You don't want to remember. You don't want to talk about it."

But talk he must. How else to convince President George W. Bush, members of Congress and the American people that he and the 10,000 surviving members of the U.S. Merchant Marine were dealt a grave injustice by the United States Government so long ago and now, to make things right, they deserve $1,000 a month tax free for as long as they live?" There is a bill in Congress – "A Belated Thank You to the Merchant Mariners of World War II Act of 2007" – that would do just that.

Bullets, Bombs and Beer

From the Revolutionary War to the war in Iraq, the merchant marine has delivered the goods. But the toughest and deadliest duty came during World War II when Berry and 250,000 men and women mariners supplied the greatest war machine in history. They hauled bombs, bullets, tanks, planes, troops, locomotives, food, fuel, even beer to every theater of war, a job so crucial that without them, mariners like to say, Americans would be speaking German and Japanese today.

With roughly half of them seeing actual combat, and the other half sailing through enemy waters, every mariner was a sitting duck for subs, mines, bombers and fighters. They suffered the highest casualty rate of any of the Armed Forces, with nearly one in 26 dying in the line of duty – some of them just offshore from Jupiter's lighthouse.

By contrast, one in 34 Marines was killed. Between February and May 1942, German U-boats sank 16 ships between Cape Canaveral and Boca Raton.

When the war ended, mariners brought millions of troops home to ticker-tape parades and a big wet kiss from the American people known as the GI Bill.

Yet the mariners received no parade, no GI Bill, no medical benefits, no small business or farm loans, no educational assistance. What they got was a stamp honoring their service and a lapel pin from the president – because they were considered civilians, not soldiers or sailors.

"We were heroes during the war," says merchant seaman *R. J. Webber*, 81, of Juno Beach. "After the war, we were forgotten."

Roosevelt, Truman, Eisenhower – All wanted the merchant mariners included in the GI Bill. But after the war, money was tight and it was easy to cut them out of the pie. For 45 years, the mariners battled with their own government until, in 1988, they were finally classified as war veterans.

But that did not even the score. The mariners want "just compensation."

"We're asking for $1,000 a month," says *Ian T. Allison*, 87, of Santa Rosa, CA, a merchant mariner who co-chairs the Just Compensation Committee. He recently testified in 2007 before the House Veterans Affairs Committee, which is was considering the bill, HR 23.

In 2007, a similar bill, co-sponsored by more than 250 members of Congress, was blocked by a single representative – Veteran Affairs chairman Steve Buyer, R-Ind.

In 2008, Buyer told the committee that there is no doubting mariners' bravery, but it is not equitable to pay them, and not other civilians who served, and "In short, thank you funds for the merchant mariners do not exist."

But with Democrats now in charge, the new chairman, Rep. *Bob Filner*, D-CA, is fully behind the effort to "find a way to compensate them, 60 years later, for their heroic deeds."

As Filner said in his opening remarks to the committee on April 18, "It is indisputable that the Allied Forces would not have been able to begin, sustain, or win World War II without the valiant service of the Merchant Marine. ... We are here today to try to give them their due in compensation. Without question, merchant mariners deserve our undying gratitude, not just in words but in deeds."

Filner says the issue is vital to national security, and he quotes America's first commander-in-chief to make his point:

President Washington got it right when he said, "The willingness with which our young people are likely to serve in any war, no matter how justified, shall be directly proportional as to how they perceive the veterans of earlier wars were treated and appreciated by their country."

The cost to taxpayers is between $40 million and $120 million a year, depending on how many WW II-era mariners apply. "But after 10 years," Allison says. "We'll all be dead."

'Too Many Words'

Webber, the Juno Beach mariner who was awarded the Combat Bar and Victory Medal for his service, has all but given up on politicians.

"It was too long ago," he says. "People don't want to listen."

But he could use the money.

"This is what worries me," he says. "I'm on Social Security. At the moment, I'm OK. But if I live too much longer, it may be difficult."

Like many mariners, Webber joined the Merchant Marine after the Navy and U.S. Coast Guard wouldn't have him. "Eye problems," he says. He wound up serving in the north Atlantic where German "wolf packs" were on the hunt. On one crossing, his ship came under attack by torpedo boats off of Antwerp while he was in the engine room. "I went up like a stupid idiot to see what was going on," he says. "That's an 18-year-old for you. I saw a lot of flares and a lot of noise. Then I went back down."

Roy Hiscock, 80, of Royal Palm Beach was rejected by the Navy because he was color blind. So he became a merchant seaman shortly after his 18th birthday. He crisscrossed the Pacific and, the day the war ended, was on a Liberty ship anchored in the harbor of Okinawa. He, too, says the money would "come in very handy."

"Most of the guys didn't have college educations," he says. "So they worked all their life. Whatever they could put aside, they put aside. After that, all you've got is Social Security."

Stanley Linn of Palm Beach Gardens, a Brooklyn chess star who once defeated Bobby Fischer before he became a world champion, attended Harvard Law School for a year before joining the merchant marine. He made five Pacific crossings and was under constant attack for three days while U.S. forces were invading the Philippine Islands. "Bombers. Surface ships with torpedoes. They came at us with planes, constantly strafing the decks of the ships. It was as dangerous as you could get during wartime. Many ships around me were destroyed."

In one attack, he lost his close friend. "He was a radio operator. A suicide bomber ran his plane into the side of the ship, the engine shook loose, ran across the deck and into the radio room, killing my friend."

He is fed up with politicians who talk about supporting the troops, but never seem to come through. "There's no question that mariners deserve this, for the same reason that members of the Armed Forces deserve it. But after all these years, I've given up. Actions have meaning. Words do not. There have been too many words."

'They're Dying Every Day'

Allison, the merchant seaman who testified before Congress, says the three-year lobbying campaign has been financed by small donations from the mariners. "Some guys send two bucks. Another guy sends 100." He believes this is the year the bill will finally pass Congress and head to President Bush's desk for his signature. "I don't think he's going to block a bill for veterans' rights," he says. "There are 10,800 guys on our mailing list. But they're dying every day. I doubt it'll be 10,000 guys still alive when they pass it."

But *Nelson Smith*, 79, of Dallas says one problem is most Washington politicians never served, never fought. "Since this thing has been ignored for so long, most of the people making the decisions (in Washington) weren't even born at the time of the war," says Smith, who joined the merchant marine when he was 17. "It's hard for them to get it straight in their head. But what would these guys have done fighting a war with no bullets, no guns, no food?" He says he believes there is only one reason why Congress has failed to act. "They would have to admit that they've been wrong for 62 years," he says.

His sister, *Jan Terrana* of West Palm Beach, has been one of the people leading the charge, writing letters to newspapers, calling members of Congress and rallying the mariners to the cause. "They deserve this," she says.

Berry, the mariner who joined the merchant marine at age 16 and watched his shipmates burn to death 65 years ago, says Americans should consider what the world would be like had the merchant marine not accomplished its mission.

"We could have lost that war," he says. "Or come out a lot worse than we did."

Family Seeks Closure From WW II Off NC Coast
Associated Press August 13, 2011

> Nearly 70 years after Capt. *Anders Johanson* was killed during WW II off the coast of North Carolina, his family is getting ready to finally pay their last respects.

> Johanson was aboard an oil tanker making its way from Texas to New Jersey when a German U-boat fired three torpedoes at the *Dixie Arrow* on March 26, 1942, bursting thousands of barrels of oil aboard the ship into flames off of North Carolina's Outer Banks. His family will revisit the site of the wreckage Wednesday.

> Survivors of the blast who were brought to Norfolk after being plucked from the sea told reporters at the time that Johanson

survived long enough to order boats and life rafts launched – which helped save 22 members of the 33-man-crew – before being engulfed in searing flames as the ship sank. His body was never recovered.

More than half a century later, his family is still trying to come to terms with his death. "He stopped in Jacksonville (FL) and asked for a destroyer escort and the destroyer came out and said, Sorry brother, everything's OK. Don't worry about it," said Johanson's grandson, Dale Revels of Orlando, FL, who along with his mother and uncle will be visiting the wreckage site for the first time as the guests of federal researchers examining World War II wrecks. "It was basically a personality failure of the American Navy."

Johanson never received the public recognition that so many others who lost their lives in World War II did. There was no funeral for his wife and two young children to honor the Swedish immigrant, who was on his last cruise for the Merchant Marine before rejoining his family in Brooklyn, NY.

Johanson's family struggled in the chaos after his death. They were uprooted from New York and had to stay with family in Beaumont, TX before a family death there left them with no home. They stayed at a boarding home in New Orleans before eventually moving in with other family in Belleview, FL where questions for the newcomers were constant.

"When I was going through high school, I didn't have a father. During that time everybody seemed to have a mother and a father and people would ask me, "Where's your father'?" said Johanson's daughter, Jeanne Johanson Revels, now 83 and living in Port Orange, FL. "They had this big campaign about loose lips sink ships in 1943 during World War II. Those two men who came to see my mother said we couldn't say anything about it. I guess it was classified information and you couldn't talk about it at all."

The sinking of merchant ships off the NC coast is now largely a historical footnote known as the Battle of the Atlantic. Federal researchers have spent the past several years examining the ship-wrecks, including the Dixie Arrow, in an effort to better protect the ships that are the only grave sites some family members will ever have. They are sponsoring Revel's expedition so that she can finally pay her respects to her father after a lifetime of searching for closure.

Famous Liberty Ships

S.S. BENJAMIN CONTEE

This is the 12th in a series of articles describing famous Liberty ships. Previous columns have described Liberty ships that became well known because of their loss to enemy action and explosion as well as those that survived the hazards of war and severe weather to continue service in peacetime. This article describes one of the seven Liberty ships that became noteworthy because it was intentionally sunk to form one of the artificial harbors at the Normandy beachhead shortly after D-day.

Planning for some type of artificial harbor at the invasion beach began shortly after the disastrous raid on Dieppe in 1942. One of the objectives of that raid had been to determine if a protected harbor could be seized without causing extensive damage, defended, and then used to offload material during an opposed landing. The Dieppe experience showed it was not feasible and that another means would be needed to move large amounts of cargo ashore when the European continent was invaded. Hence, the need to develop an artificial harbor, called a "Mulberry," was born.

The original concept was to form breakwaters off the five invasion beaches by scuttling ships in a line to form barriers called "*Gooseberries.*" Four obsolete warships and 55 merchant ships were used, including seven Liberty ships. BENJAMIN CONTEE was one of the Liberty ships used to form "*Gooseberry 1,*" having been damaged earlier in the war, and was typical of the other ships selected for this project. The Liberty ships JAMES W. MARSHALL, JAMES IREDELL, GEORGE S. WATSON, MATT W. RANSOM, ARTEMUS WARD, and GEORGE M. CHILDS were also used. The ships were manned by volunteer crews and sailed or towed to Normandy where they were placed in position by tugs and then scuttled using an explosive charge.

BENJAMIN CONTEE was built by Delta Shipbuilding Company and launched in June 1942. Records are not clear but she was apparently converted to a "limited capacity troop transport" later that year somewhere in the Mediterranean Theater where she was operating. The conversion occurred prior to the formal program that began in American yards the following year and which would include JOHN W. BROWN. CONTEE was making the short voyage from Bona to Oran, Algeria with 1,800 Italian POWs and a security detachment aboard. Just before midnight on August 16, 1943, she was attacked by a German torpedo bomber that avoided early detection by gliding in to attack the ship. The torpedo blew a large hole in the hull at #one and #two holds, killing almost 300 POWs.

A line of sunken ships forms a Gooseberry breakwater off Utah Beach,
during the Normandy Invasion June 1944.
National Archives, Washington D.C.

The ship initially settled by the head until the after holds were counter-flooded to bring her back to an even keel. Temporary repairs were made at Gibraltar before the ship sailed to New York for further repairs in January 1944. In February she sailed in a convoy to Southampton, England. After offloading there, she was earmarked for use in a Gooseberry.

The CONTEE was sailed to Normandy, manned by volunteers, to be positioned and scuttled off the American invasion beaches, designated Omaha and Utah. There she came under heavy shell fire and was abandoned by the tugs that were maneuvering her into the Gooseberry line. By good fortune, the ship settled in the proper position when scuttled.

The Liberty ships' GEORGE S. WASSON and MATT W. RANSOM were part of the same Gooseberry.

Ironically, a violent northeasterly storm swept through the area from June 19-22 destroying most of the artificial harbors off the American beaches. By that time the beachhead was secure and the Mulberry harbor off the British beaches (Juno, Gold, and Sword) remained in operation until French ports were captured and could be used to handle cargo.

H.M.S. "Centurion"

Aerial View: Gooseberry 2 off St Laurent during the storm on June 20 1944.
Look at the waves breaking over the ship indicated with an arrow.

Selected Articles of Interest

The Jewish Citizen
World War II-era Merchant Mariners Seek Compensation
for Lost G. I. Bill

Thursday, August 21, 2008

By Donald H. Harrison

SAN DIEGO – Sheldon Merel, the cantor emeritus of Congregation Beth Israel, is among the thousands of men and women now in their 80s who risked their lives in service of the United States during World War II but were excluded from receiving the GI benefits that for many veterans after World War II were passports to the middle class.

The veterans who were included in the GI Bill of Rights - whether they faced enemy fire or stayed stateside in an office job - were eligible to receive low interest loans to buy homes, go to college, train for new jobs, and, in short, to have the government help them begin their lives anew in recognition for the service that they gave to their country.

Those who had served in the regular U. S. Armed Forces - the Army, Navy and the Marines - were the lucky veterans eligible for the GI Bill of Rights. In contrast, Merel and approximately 10,000 of his compatriots still living had served in the U. S. Merchant Marine, and their sacrifices were not rewarded. They were the "civilians" who risked their lives in the war theater, steaming in famed "Liberty Ships" through waters infested with enemy submarines to supply U. S. Armed forces and their allies with military equipment, grain, fuel, even personnel. Thousands of Merchant Mariners were killed or maimed when German or Japanese torpedoes sunk their ships.

Typically, Navy gunners served with the civilian Merchant Marine on the Liberty Ships, with both categories of fighters facing identical dangers. But when the war ended, those who were Navy personnel received the G. I. Bill; while those who were "civilians" were left out.

Why this happened is a matter of debate. Some say it was because Merchant Mariners often received higher salaries than Armed Forces personnel - a contention that Merchant Mariners contest, pointing out that they didn't receive salaries for the times before and after their voyages, only when they were on their ships.

Some suggest it was because Merchant Mariners were not ordered into combat as members of the Armed Forces were; it was the Mariners' choice whether or not to accept assignment on a ship. And when a voyage was completed, it was their choice to sign on for another voyage or turn to other civilian pursuits. Armed Forces personnel had no such choice.

As a Third Engineer, Merel stood a watch of four hours over the ship's reciprocating engines, then had eight hours off duty. His first voyage brought guns, armored tanks and food to Naples, Italy. His second tour, on the same ship, was to Southern France. Thereafter, he signed onto an oil tanker. He said that whereas Liberty ships usually crossed the Atlantic in well-protected convoys, with the trips taking 30 days at the slow speed of 10 knots; the oiler was at least twice as fast, and able to outrun submarines. So it crossed the ocean without a convoy. "We went to England, and unloaded the oil, and it was a real fast turnover," he recalled. "We loaded seawater for ballast as there was nothing to take back, and we headed home." Then he went to upgrade school, passed an examination, and was promoted to Second Engineer.

From his home in New York, Merel transferred to Galveston, Texas, where he signed onto a grain ship. He still can remember their cargo to Bizerte, Algeria, and while there, he suffered an attack of appendicitis. He was treated by a doctor of the French Foreign Legion, who had him transferred to a French naval hospital for removal of the appendix. "I was there for about two weeks, and no one spoke English at the French naval hospital," recalled Merel. Patients were allowed to have their spouses live at the hospital, and the husband of one female patient spoke a little English. "They gave me ether, and I was a little agitated, and he said to me, in broken English, 'do not worry, for you it is all over.' I shall always remember that."

After recuperating in Tunis, Merel shipped back to the United States, the war having ended. "The moment my ship hit the port in the United States my pay stopped," he said. "I was given an honorable discharge and I went back to college (CCNY). My dream had been to go to a college out of state, but with no GI Bill of Rights, there was no way that I or my family could afford it."

In his four voyages across the Atlantic, Merel was one of the lucky ones, never having come under hostile fire. Another Jewish San Diegan, Herman "Hank" Rosen, was far from being so lucky in his Merchant Marine career. As described in his book, Gallant Ship, Brave Men, Rosen's Liberty ship, the SS John Drayton, had been torpedoed on April 21, 1943 off the coast of Africa. He was among 24 Merchant Mariners who got into a lifeboat, but after a 30-day ordeal, only five of them survived.

The men in the lifeboat broiled during the day, and froze at night. There was insufficient food. Rosen had lost 50 pounds - from 140 to 90 -by the time he was rescued. Nineteen of his shipmates had died of malnutrition and exposure.

In his testimony before the Senate Committee on Veteran Affairs, Filner stated: "The Merchant Mariners became the forgotten service.

For four decades, no effort was made to recognize the contribution made by this branch of the Armed Services. The fact that Merchant Seamen had borne arms during wartime in the defense of their country seemed not to matter. The result of being left out of the G.I. Bill meant that the Mariners could not buy a home or go to college, as their counterparts in service were doing. Without college education, the jobs that were open to them paid significantly less and was less fulfilling in many cases. It was impossible for them to become a doctor, lawyer, teacher, engineer. And it was impossible to purchase a home, one of the stepping stones to the middle class. My father was a World War II veteran and his ability to buy a home came from the G.I. Bill."

First Voyage to Sea 1942
Vince Patterson (Tri-State Chapter, AMMV)

War broke out between the United States and Japan on December 7, 1941. I was 15 years old and lived in the port city of New Orleans. As much as I wanted to fight for my country, I knew that the armed forces would not accept me because I was too young.

In January of 1942, I turned 16 and asked my parents to sign for me to join the United States Navy. From a young age, I had always wanted to be a sailor as was my grandfather. When my parents turned me down for the Navy, I found another way to become a sailor.

At 16, my parents agreed to let me join the United States Merchant Marine. I told them it would not be dangerous (little did I know). I did not go to a maritime school as most of the young recruits did. I passed my Coast Guard physical and received my seaman papers in June of 1942.

In July 1942, I was assigned to a new Liberty Ship, the S.S. Mirabeau B. Lamar in Houston, Texas. The ship was still in the shipyard and we were the first to crew it. We left Houston and sailed for New Orleans to load cargo.

A day before we arrived at Southwest Pass, the troop ship Robert E. Lee was torpedoed and sunk by a German submarine. This was July 30, 1942 and she went under the waves in 15 minutes. There were only a few survivors.

As we approached the Southwest Pass of the mouth of the Mississippi River, two of our Destroyer Escorts (DEs) began dropping depth charges off our port bow. Depth charges are high explosive canisters that can sink a submarine. They pick up sonar soundings from a submarine that is stalking our ship. Underwater radio signals sent out will bounce back when they strike an object. Both DEs were gradually working the submarine into the shallow water of the coastline and the Louisiana marshes.

I was on deck watching all that was going on. Being a kid of 16 this was extremely exciting stuff, never thinking of the horror that was being played out on the submarine that the DEs were stalking.

The submarine would not or could not surface. A twin engine plane from Alvin Calendar Airfield at Belle Chase, Louisiana helped with the search. The plane flew over a spot near the two destroyer escorts and dropped a floating smoke flare and flew off. In a minute or two it returned and dropped a large bomb. This in turn seemed to blow the bottom out of the Gulf of Mexico with a tall geyser of mud, debris and water and, I assumed, parts of the submarine.

We now headed up the Mississippi River and stopped at Pilot Town, a small distance up from the mouth of the river. Pilot Town is a couple of houses built on stilts above the marsh, where pilots stay between bringing ships up and down the river. A pilot was taken aboard our ship and we headed up river about 90 miles to New Orleans.

Upon reaching the city, our steering gear went haywire and we were unable to steer the ship. It takes a long time to stop a ship making headway, even going up river against the current. Both anchors were dropped and, with the engine going full astern, we still plowed into the dock. We hit and crunched the dock between two ships. One was a British ship loaded with munitions. Great for us and the city of New Orleans that we did not blow up the town.

I get to visit with my family, as I suspect we will be on a long voyage. After several weeks loading cargo, we sailed for the Gulf of Mexico. We joined with a convoy of ships. Our convoy is going through the Caribbean Sea and headed for the island of Trinidad. We could hear depth charges but no ships were sunk.

We had shore leave in Trinidad and this was the first time I had seen people sleeping and living on the streets. Our stay in Trinidad was short. I got to see a small portion of Trinidad and visit the USO Club. We danced in a conga line but had to leave the pretty girls ashore. Time to weigh anchor and go to war, we were on our way to Cape Town, South Africa. We had no destroyer escorts to protect us. We were on our own. We had four TWENTY-mm guns and one three-inch gun forward. On our stern we had an old five-inch gun left over from World War I. We loaded the power bags with a ram rod and a projectile.

There were German "Raiders" disguised as merchant ships that carried many more and larger guns than we did. German submarines were also along our route. We were lucky and arrived at Cape Town without incident. Another ship, the West Chetac that left Trinidad with us did not arrive; it was way overdue. It did not make it. Many of the crew had friends aboard her. The West Chetac was sunk shortly after leaving Trinidad on September 24, 1942 by U-175.

The ship sank in two minutes. Twenty-two crew and nine Navy Armed Guards were lost, including the Captain.

Cape Town is a beautiful city, located below Table Top mountain on the southern tip of Africa. We got to visit some of the sights and out-lying villages. We ate at a café on Table Top mountain. The people were friendly.

Large black fellows of the Zulu tribe unloaded our ship. Some had fancy, round, painted spools in their ears. Many had rods through the bottom part of their noses and scar markings on their faces. Their bare feet looked two inches thick. Some of the people and their customs had not changed in many decades.

With part of our cargo unloaded, we were now on our way to Port Elizabeth located on the east coast of South Africa. We arrived and, though our shore leave was short, we managed to see some of the city.

Our next scheduled stop was Durban, South Africa but we became lost. We spent the last three or more days by dead reckoning. We were looking for the entrance to the harbor at Durban. The weather was very bad, and we could not take a sighting with our sextants. Japanese submarines patrolled these waters. The Japanese were mean adversaries; they spared no one.

When the weather cleared, we learned we were not too far off course. We arrived at Durban and unloaded for four days.

Next we headed up through the South Atlantic ocean to Surinam, located in the northeastern part of South America. Our ship was a hundred miles from the South American shore, and night was falling when our ship was attacked by a submarine. The Navy gun crew gave a good account of themselves and drove the submarine off. The sub may have fired a torpedo at us, but since it was night, we could not know.

We arrived the next morning at Paramaribo in Surinam and continued up river to Paranam to load bauxite (an aluminum ore). Our next stop was Trinidad to top off the cargo holds with additional bauxite.

The ship was then on the last leg of the journey, and we dropped anchor in sight of the Statue of Liberty in New York harbor, just in time for a white Christmas 1942.

The Pineapple
by Vince Patterson

Our ship, the SS James Kyron Walker, unloaded general cargo at the ports of La Havre and Rouen, France. Our orders now read to proceed to Paramaribo, in the Nation of Surinam, then up the river to the mines of Paranam to load bauxite.

Surinam is located between Guyana and French Guiana on the upper eastern portion of South America. Bauxite is a reddish ore that aluminum is derived from. Ships have been coming up the river from Paramaribo to the bauxite mines for years, especially during the war years, when most aircraft were made of aluminum.

Ships can only take two-thirds of the bauxite cargo in their holds. The river is not deep enough to fully load the ship. Ships will top off their cargo from a large bauxite storage hulk the sailors call "Dirty Dick" in the port of Trinidad. That nickname comes from the qualities of the bauxite ore when loading. The dust will invade just about every crack and crevasse; it will get into your clothes, food and person. A red powder will envelope the ship.

When they load the ship, it is moved forward and backward in order to load it on an even keel. The ship's whistle is blown each time the ship is moved. Sandy and I were off watch, just leaning on the ship's rail looking at the jungle. The shadows of the jungle looked a lot cooler than the hot ship. We decided to walk down a dirt path that led from the dock into the jungle. Maybe we would come across some bananas or mangoes growing wild. We plodded along for about ten or more minutes and came upon a steel structure. It was about 75 feet in length with a tin roof and the sides were open three quarters of the way up. Inside this structure were small rail cars full of red ore. There were eight natives that worked in the mine, some standing and some sitting down. One of the workers had in front of him a very large, ripe, juicy looking pineapple. We had never seen a pineapple that large. We wanted that big, juicy pineapple.

Both Sandy and I smoked, and all we had to bargain with was a pack of cigarettes. We had no money. However, no amount of haggling would acquire us that large, ripe, juicy pineapple. As we were bargaining, the ship's whistle blew twice and the worker with the pineapple said, "Ship go now." "No," I replied, "It is just moving forward to load another hold." Again, he repeated, "Ship go." Sandy said, "Maybe he's right." By the time we found the path and made our way out of the jungle and back to the dock, it was empty. The ship had gone. We could see the ship's stern as it headed down the river.

We were in the jungles of Surinam, with no money and no idea how to get back to Paramaribo. Maybe there was an American Council office in Paramaribo, if we could only get there. It would take days of walking, even if we knew the way.

We again entered the jungle and happened upon a dirt road. Our instinct was to walk in the direction that the ship had taken in the river. After walking for about ten or more minutes, two buildings came in sight, one on each side of the road. On our left was a small house holding the office to the mines. It looked like no one was in the office although we did not try the door. On the right side was a small general store that had a rickety wooden porch with an old red coke machine. The porch on the general store looked shady and inviting so we sat down on the stairs. Our throats were dry and we looked longingly at the coke machine, but that was out of the question.

After fifteen or more minutes, the door to the office opened and a young man stepped into the yard. He looked at us and came over laughing and said, "It looks like you fellows missed your ship." "Yes," we replied, "We did indeed miss our ship." Then the young man said, "A local bus is due to arrive in about ten minutes and it will eventually take you into Paramaribo." We answered, "That's well and good but we have no money to pay the fare." Again he laughed and told us he would pay our fare as it was not very much. How lucky can you get! Thanks was the order of the day.

We could hear the bus before we could see it. The bus arrived amid a clanging of tin, sounding of brakes, horn and large cloud of red dust. The color of the bus at one time might have been dark blue, but because of the rust and dirt, it was hard to tell. Like a bus you might see in the movies, the seats were well worn and most of the padding gone. It had no glass in the windows and the road dust filled every inch. The bus was crowded with people taking their chickens, a small piglet and various types of produce to the marketplace in Paramaribo. We were so glad to be on our way to the city, and we would have ridden on the roof.

At times, the road ran parallel to the river and the terrain was very hilly. As we came to a clearing on some of the hills, we can see our ship heading down the river but could never catch it. A couple of hours passed and we arrived at Paramaribo. The bus went right to the marketplace located on the bank of the river. The location was handy for the natives coming to market in their boats and dugouts.

Luck is with us and the ship is at anchor in the river. The Chief Steward was taking on fresh supplies. We walked up to the launch they were loading, and the steward asked, "Where the hell did you two come from? I know you didn't come ashore with our supply boat." "Stew," I said, "We did not come over on the supply boat. We were sidetracked in the jungle by a big pineapple. But you can bet we will be going back on your supply launch."

Sandy and I stood on the dock watching the people load the supplies. There were a lot of fresh vegetables and greens. Two men set a large box without a top in the launch. We looked at each other and started laughing. Inside the box were "big, ripe, juicy Pineapples."

Explorers Find Downed German U-Boat Off Massachusetts Nearly 70 Years After It Sank
Coast Guard-manned Destroyer Escorts
USS Joyce (DE-317) & Peterson (DE-152) Sink the U-550
Published July 27, 2012, Associated Press
by Scott Price

By 1944, German submarines no longer prowled unimpeded through Allied sea lanes. The massive increase in the numbers of new merchant and escort vessels, long-range antisubmarine aircraft, and technological advances such as radar, sonar, and the evolution of antisubmarine tactics that utilized all of these new advances were factors that blunted the Nazi's U-boat offensive. A few U-boats, however, still attempted to interdict the precious convoys. Allied escort vessels, many Coast Guard-manned, remained vigilant.

On the afternoon of 15 April 1944, the 28 merchant ships of the fast-tanker convoy CU-21 departed New York harbor for Great Britain. Poor weather conditions prohibited them from forming up into their assigned positions within the convoy, which they usually did well outside of the harbor. So instead they simply formed two columns and steamed on through the night. Their escorts for the voyage, six destroyer escorts, had rendezvoused by this time and formed up around the merchantmen, much like sheepdogs guarding a flock, their sonars probing the rough water for any sign of intruders.

Fortunately the weather cleared the next morning and the convoy's commodore, Captain E. H. Tillman, USN, the man in charge of all of the merchant ships in the convoy, ordered the merchant ships to take their appropriate places. Despite the care with which the escorts took in protecting their charges, an unannounced observer watched with interest as the large tankers maneuvered into their assigned convoy positions. The U-550, one of three U-boats that dared venture into the North Atlantic that spring, was on its first combat patrol. She had lain in wait outside New York harbor for just such an opportunity. Its young commanding officer, Kapitanleutnant Klaus Hanert, saw what every U-boat commander looked for: a straggler. This merchant ship, a tanker with a full cargo of aviation fuel, was well behind the forming convoy. What luck! Not only was she a straggler, but she was also one of the most valuable targets any U-boat could hope to attack.

As the tanker sailed ever closer to the submerged U-boat, Hanert's crew prepared their attack. He checked the range and bearing to the target, and this data was fed into the torpedo aiming computer which then prepared the torpedo for its run. Once ready, Hanert gave the order to fire. A little after 0800 the single torpedo hit the port side of the SS Pan Pennsylvania, the largest tanker in the world at that time. It carried a highly combustible cargo of 140,000 barrels of 80-octane aviation fuel, a fact not lost on its 50-man crew or the 31 members of her Naval Armed Guard.

Many men panicked and leapt into the water while others attempted to launch a lifeboat without waiting for the order to abandon ship or for the Pan Pennsylvania to come to a complete stop. The lifeboat capsized and spilled the men into the frigid water. Luckily the cargo did not explode but only began to catch fire. But the explosion did cut communications between the bridge and the engine room. The tanker's master sent the chief engineer to check on the conditions in the engine room while he informed the convoy commander of his predicament. He then searched the ship to make sure that no remaining crewmen were trapped as the huge tanker began to settle by the stern.

In an effort to evade an inevitable counterattack by the escorts, Hanert attempted to place his submerged U-boat near the sinking tanker, hoping it would mask his presence. Unbeknownst to him, however, the escorts were also heading in that direction, as Kenner immediately ordered the Joyce to retrieve the survivors. He then ordered USS Peterson and the Gandy to screen the rescue effort, and the three destroyer escorts broke formation and sailed toward the stricken tanker, all with their sonar equipment actively pinging the area. The situation on board the Pan Pennsylvania worsened. The chief engineer inspected the engine room and saw what the men feared the most. A fire had broken out and was spreading. The engineer reported back to the tanker's master who then gave the order to abandon ship. The tanker continued to settle by the stern and developed a list to port but the crew managed to launch two lifeboats and three life rafts before the ocean's surface began to wash over the tanker's large deck.

Joyce hove to near the doomed ship, and its crew quickly went to work retrieving the survivors. There were so many, in fact, that Peterson had to lend a hand. *Joyce's* crew pulled 31 merchant marines from the lifeboats and rafts and *Peterson's* crew saved 25, but 25 others remained unaccounted for. The tanker continued to settle and then slowly capsized. As *Joyce* prepared to get underway, her sonar operator obtained a contact at 1,800 yards. Hanert, growing uneasy so near a sinking ship, had attempted to slowly and quietly move away from the drowning behemoth. *U-550's* engineer later told interrogators, "We waited for your ship to leave; soon we could hear nothing so we thought the escort vessels had gone; but as soon as we started to move – bang!"

Joyce's commanding officer, Lieutenant Commander Robert Wilcox, USCG, gave orders to prepare to attack and brought the warship to flank speed. *Joyce* radioed the other two destroyer escorts about the contact as her crew prepared to drop depth charges. *Gandy* formed up behind *Joyce* to carry out a synchronized attack. *Peterson* sailed close behind her sisters. As *Joyce* passed over the sound contact, her crew dropped 13 depth charges, all set to a shallow setting. In a perfectly timed and executed attack the depth charges bracketed the submerged submarine and exploded, literally blowing the *U-550* out of the water. The depth charges were so well placed, reported another German survivor, that one depth charge actually bounced off the submerged U-boat's deck plating before it exploded.

The sailors saw the U-boat's bow break the surface and both *Gandy's* and *Peterson's* commanding officers gave the order to ram. At the same time, the three destroyer escorts opened fire on the hapless Germans but the two Coast Guard-manned warships ceased firing as the *Gandy* unadvisedly sailed between them and the submarine. *Peterson* veered off as *Gandy* closed with the German submarine.

Gandy slammed into the *U-550* abaft the conning tower, damaging the U-boat further and *Peterson* fired two depth charges from her

"K" guns, which exploded along the side of the German submarine. Once Gandy was clear, all three destroyer escorts again opened fire, preventing the German crew from attempting to man their deck guns. Nevertheless a number of U-boatmen attempted just that and were cut down as they exited their hatches. When Gandy ceased firing, more Germans attempted to man the after machine gun and actually managed to open fire briefly before the concentrated fire from all three destroyer escorts mowed each one down and laid waste to the conning tower.

U-550 continued taking on water and dipped lower within the sea. The surviving U-boatmen, realizing their submarine was doomed, first set their scuttling charges and attempted to abandon ship. The charges exploded quickly, and the U-boat quickly settled by the stern and then sank beneath the waves, trapping most of the crew within its hull. The destroyer escorts ceased firing and sailed in close to rescue the few survivors, men who they were attempting to kill only a few moments before. Joyce managed to pull thirteen German sailors from the water, including U-550's commander, but the rest of the U-boat's crew went to the bottom with their submarine. As the three destroyer escorts sailed back to the convoy, the Gandy's crew patched the damage they received when they rammed U-550. The now capsized Pan Pennsylvania lay against the horizon, a solemn reminder of just how deadly the Battle of the Atlantic still was. The smoking hulk was sunk by gunfire two days later.

One of the rescued U-boatmen, Heinrich Wenz, later died from his wounds. LCDR Wilcox conducted a funeral service and then committed Wenz's body to the sea. The convoy continued on to Britain, despite the loss of the Pan Pennsylvania, and arrived there unscathed. In a gruesome side script to the story, apparently some of the German crewmen survived the sinking of their U-boat in their forward watertight compartments. Over the next few hours or days they attempted to eject from their sunken submarine to reach the surface with their escape equipment, but unfortunately perished in the attempt. A few of their bodies were recovered floating off the coast a few days later, fueling speculation that some Germans actually made it to shore along the U.S. Coast.

Forty-four Germans were killed, and 25 aboard the tanker died.

National Maritime Day

May 22, 2007

May 22 is National Maritime Day, established by Presidential Proclamation in 1933. It marks the day when, in 1819, the SS Savannah sailed from Savannah, GA to Liverpool, England making the first successful crossing of the Atlantic Ocean by a ship using steam propulsion. Each year in Dania Beach, Florida, on this day, the men and women currently serving in the American Merchant Marine are honored, along with the many seamen who lost their lives in World War II, Korea, Vietnam and the Persian Gulf Conflicts.

Here is our contribution to that honorable ceremony:

THE MERCHANT MARINE
By *Edgar A. Guest*

We seldom get their names, In spite of all they do.
They're merely mentioned in the press "As members of the crew"
Yet they're the men whose courage, arms and clothes, equips and feeds,
The boys in every battle zone Who do the glorious deeds.
We speak of them as Merchant Men, Yet when they once set out,
No matter where their course may run, Death follows them about.
They're stalked by death from port to port, when once the anchor is weighed,
From master down to cabin boy.
They're Sailors unafraid, They know the lurking submarines,
They've seen them break the wave. And still with little means to fight,
The cruel odds they brave, Sometimes they are struck in the dead of night,
And into rafts they fall – And drift about and pray to God,
To save them all.
We think of them as Merchant Men, But when the war is won,

They too must share the pride, For duty nobly done,
And when the world is free once more, And home the boys from sea,
When from the foxholes come, The lads with us once more to be,
When from the skies the boys slip down, Let us all remember then,
The courage of the Yankee youth, Who sailed as MERCHANT MEN.

Thank you NVP Joe Colon for this beautiful piece of culture. As an adjunct to the above, this came across my desk recently: Pope Benedict, during the month of June, prayed for all of us. He said, "We especially lift up sailors and all those who work in the sea." He continued, "Lord please protect every sailor and all those involved in Maritime Activities."

Important Laws

A few laws have shaped the development of the U. S. merchant marine. Chief among them is the "Seamen's Act of 1915," the "Merchant Marine Act of 1920" (commonly referred to as the "Jones Act"), and the "Merchant Marine Act of 1936.

The Seamen's Act of 1915

The Seaman's Act significantly improved working conditions for American seamen. The brainchild of International Seamen's Union president Andrew Furuseth, the Act was sponsored in the Senate by Robert Marion La Follette and received significant support from Secretary of Labor William B. Wilson.

Among other things, the Act:

1. Abolished the practice of imprisonment for seamen who deserted their ship;
2. Reduced the penalties for disobedience;
3. Regulated working hours both at sea and in port;
4. Established minimum food quality standards;
5. Regulated the payment of wages;

6. Required specific levels of safety, particularly the provision of lifeboats;
7. Required a minimum percentage of the seamen aboard a vessel to be qualified Able Seamen; and
8. Required a minimum of 75% of the seamen aboard a vessel to understand the language spoken by the officers.

The Act's passage was attributed to labor union lobbying, increased labor tensions immediately before World War I, and elevated public consciousness of safety at sea due to the sinking of the RMS Titanic three years prior.

The Jones Act

The "Merchant Marine Act of 1920," often called The "Jones Act," required U.S.-flagged vessels to be built in the United States, owned by U.S. citizens, and documented ("flagged") under the laws of the United States. It also required that all officers and 75% of the crew be U. S. citizens. Vessels satisfying these requirements comprised the "Jones Act Fleet," and only these vessels were allowed to engage in "cabotage," or carrying passengers or cargo between two U.S. ports.

Another important aspect of the Act is that it allowed injured sailors to obtain compensation from their employers for the negligence of the owner, the captain, or fellow members of the crew.

The Merchant Marine Act

The Merchant Marine Act of 1936 was enacted "to further the development and maintenance of an adequate and well-balanced American merchant marine, to promote the commerce of the United States, to aid in the national defense, to repeal certain former legislation, and for other purposes.

Specifically, the Act established the United States Maritime Commission and required a United States Merchant Marine that consisted of U.S.-built, U.S.-flagged, U.S.-crewed and U.S.-owned vessels capable of carrying all domestic and a substantial portion of foreign water-borne commerce which could serve as a naval auxiliary in time of war or national emergency.

The Act also established federal subsidies for the construction and operation of merchant ships. Two years after the Act was passed, the U.S. Merchant Marine Cadet Corps, the forerunner to the United States Merchant Marine Academy, was established.

Noted U.S. Merchant Mariners

Ian T. Allison and Eddie Albert

Eddie Albert, star of stage and screen, was made Honorary Member of the North Bay Chapter of the AMMV in Santa Rosa, CA, at age 95. Ian Allison, Co-Chair of the AMMV Just Compensation Committee and a 30-year friend of Eddie Albert, said "Eddie was a real hero at the Bloody

Battle of Tarawa in the South Pacific. In command of an LCM, Eddie transported, under heavy fire, innumerable loads of wounded American Marines from the beach of Tarawa to off-shore hospital ships."

Eddie's own statement of support on December 7, 2002 was: "It is my belief, without the U.S. Merchant Marine and their dedicated seamen, America and her Allies could never have won the war."

Songwriter and lyricist *Jack Lawrence* was a mariner during World War II and wrote the official United States Merchant Marine song, "Heave Ho! My Lads, Heave Ho!" while a young lieutenant stationed at Sheepshead Bay, Brooklyn, in 1943.

Fictional Accounts

In animations and cartoons:
Popeye was a merchant mariner before joining first the U.S. Coast Guard, and then the U.S. Navy.

Onscreen:

Action in the North Atlantic is a 1943 film featuring Humphrey Bogart, Raymond Massey, and Alan Hale, Sr. as merchant mariners fighting the Battle of the Atlantic in WW II;
The Long Voyage Home starring John Wayne;
The Men Who Sailed the Liberty Ships, television documentary.

Notes

The United States Merchant Marine Academy in Kings Point also changed its admission policy in 1974, becoming the first national academy (two years ahead of Navy, Air Force or Coast Guard) to enroll women. Historically, women who wanted to ship out encountered prejudice and superstition. Their hands-on seafaring experiences were largely limited to voyages as the captain's wife or daughter. Subsequently, some women chose to ship out by disguising themselves as men.

A Serious Political Mistake

It was a severe, critical, strategic, political mistake for the unions to make in drawing the ire and fire of armed forces leaders. This blunder came back to haunt union membership after the war when military people belittled the contributions of merchant seamen during the war and actively lobbied against benefits for them. Long skilled at maneuvering in political waters, the Navy managed to exert de facto authority over the merchant service all during the war. The Navy also gained by the U.S. Coast Guard becoming responsible for the inspection of merchant ships' seaworthiness and for the examination, licensing and certification of Merchant Marine personnel.

Stormy political waters swirled around the Merchant Marine during and after WW II. At Midway in 1942, there was a report that each member of the crew of the SS Nira Luckenbach had received $1,000 and refused to unload war materials on Sunday unless they were paid overtime. The truth was that there were no facilities and manpower capable of unloading the hazardous cargo of bombs and barrels of gasoline at Midway atoll. The ship's captain proceeded to unload as best he could with his small crew. No Merchant Marine crew ever refused to unload their ship during WW II.

Another tall tale originated from Kuluk Harbor, Alaska, and involved the SS Thomas Jefferson, a Liberty ship. Reportedly, a U.S. destroyer approached a docked merchant ship and asked for a line to be thrown to them. Allegedly, no one responded. They had already done their eight hours of work and had gone ashore. This story proved false as well. The trouble stemmed from the animosity between the master and an officer on the Navy destroyer after the master demanded a receipt for the fuel oil the destroyer had received.

Despite the published famous quotes of admiration of the Merchant Marine by our top leaders, Presidents Roosevelt and Truman; Generals Eisenhower, Marshall, MacArthur and Vandergrift; Admirals King, Land and Nimitz, our casualties of one in every 26, the highest of any service, including the Marine Corps, the Merchant Mariners to this day are deemed draft dodgers, drunks, not veterans, free loader seekers and many, many more derogatory and detractive descriptions. These are lies, lies and damn lies, and the Merchant Mariners are victims of all.

The Army, Navy and Marine Corps fought and won their many battles and had heavy casualties in WW II. However, it was well known by our top commanding admirals and generals that without the war materials delivered to their fighting men at the right time by the Merchant Mariners, WW II would almost certainly have been lost to the Axis powers. Europe was facing starvation when President Roosevelt sent our Liberty ships across the Atlantic under his "Lend Lease" program.

In evaluating the service of the Merchant Marine to the military and naval establishments, the opinion of the men in command should be considered. On November 2, 1945, Fleet Admiral Ernest J. King, Commander-in-Chief of the U.S. Navy & Chief of Naval Operations, wrote to Admiral Emory S. Land, War Shipping Administrator: "During the past 3.5 years, the Navy has been dependent on the Merchant Marine to supply our far-flung fleet and bases. Without this support, the Navy could not have accomplished its mission. Consequently, it is fitting they share in our success as they did in our trials. The Merchant Marine is a strong bulwark of national defense in peace and war and a buttress to a sound national economy."

"A large Merchant Marine is not only an important national resource; it is, in being, an integral part of the country's armed might during times of crisis. During WW II, this precept has been proven. I take pleasure in expressing the Navy's heartfelt thanks to the officers and men of the Merchant Marine for their magnificent support during WW II."

Seaman's Bill of Rights Crashed on the Rocks in 1947:

Captain Warren G. Leback said the Merchant Seamen were "too busy fighting the war when those political machinations occurred." That bill was introduced sometime before FDR died on April 12, 1945. We think it might have been introduced by Congressman Otis Bland of VA. Admirals Emory S. Land and Telfair Knight worked to get the bill introduced. Congressional hearings were delayed until after the war ended in the Pacific, and that was in mid-August, 1945. On May 19, 1945, MARAD issued a flyer warning that they must continue to sail or they would not be eligible for their GI Bill when it is passed by Congress. That flyer was placed on all ships and posted in the mess halls. MARAD was terrified that the Merchant Mariners would no longer go to sea now that the Germans had surrendered. A very few did quit.

Harry Truman was President then, and he was not interested and had no time to support that bill despite his Merchant Marine highest casualty list and a major reason the US and our allies won WW II.

Perry Adams recalls, as best he can now, that the first hearing was May 10, 1946 due to Admiral Edmond J. Moran inviting him to accompany him to Washington for the hearing. We heard later that the hearings were all disapprovals, discrediting and ruinous to the Merchant Mariners' one opportunity to be recognized and honored as a combat veteran with a benefit. Almost all of the charges made against those testifying for the Merchant Mariners were lies. Our bill never made it to the floor for an up or down vote in either the House or Senate. It died in Committee.

We believe the only person who testified on our behalf was Rear Admiral Telfair Knight. We were opposed by the War Department, American Legion, VFW (Veterans of Foreign Wars) and even the Maritime unions.

The SUP (Seaman's Union of the Pacific) President, Harry Lundberg testified against the bill saying, "We will take care of our boys."

No Jobs

By the end of 1946, three quarters of the Merchant Mariners had left the seas as there were no jobs to be had. Ships were being laid up or sold to foreign countries and even our former enemies –Germany, Italy and Japan. The prices paid for our thousands of ships no longer needed were near nothing compared to our cost of building them. However, most were sold to our wartime allies – Korea, Greece and South American countries.

Either Admiral Land or Knight was found to have written a long report to President Roosevelt outlining the needs of Merchant seamen and their families. It told of the need of health care for both the seamen and their families and educational benefits to train them for jobs ashore, as many had joined the Merchant Marine as school dropouts, and only a few would ever have the funds to buy a farm or home. The result of this 1946 anti-Merchant Marine, cruel and outrageous un-American legislative policy in the US Congress has carried on until the publication of this book. We leaders and officers of the AMMV found that we could not get the Chapter's members to contact their Congress person, and never their Senator, relative to cosponsoring our Bill HR23. They never had an education, job or position that allowed them to feel comfortable in calling or writing Congressional offices and dealing with the staffers, and they would not do it. They just hoped that, like on ships, their officers would handle the problem.

WW II Merchant Mariners Ten-Year Effort Does Not Pay Off

Veteran's Status Granted Has Amounted to Nothing of Value and Is The Same Today

1977 – Organization of Public Law 95-202 GI Improvement Act was introduced in Congress by Senator Goldwater and benefitted Women's Air Service Pilots (WASP) only. He was an Air Force Reserve general who was in charge of the WW II ferry pilots who sponsored a Senate version of the bill. There was at least 15 bills introduced in Congress on their behalf. This was a political plum extended during women's lib movement, although the criterion was not completely met. Male ferry pilots and Guam combat control, as well as sundry other groups, were also granted VA benefits under the same law.

1978 – Charles Dana Gibson filed his first application to include those in the Army Transport Service.

1980 – Gibson's ATS application was denied. With the help of voluminous MARAD's archival researchers, Joan S. McAvoy filed an application to include the Merchant Marine. Those other groups (except the Women's Auxiliary Corps) were small in number. The thousands of potential Merchant Mariners who would be eligible for benefits and the tremendous political opposition by the American Legion resulted in a refusal of the ATS application.

1982 – Applications for cadets of the US Merchant Marine Academy who served at sea during WW II, which included combat zones, were denied. (122 were killed in action. The USMMA is the only federal academy among the five that sends their cadets into combat.)

1984 – Secretary of the Air Force provided a token gesture with approval of application of the US Army Transport crew.

1985 – Both McAvoy's and Gibson's applications were denied. Gibson reflected that the sight of the big picture had been lost and that the Merchant Marine is entirely controlled by the War Shipping Administration and armed by the Navy, which is true.

1986 – Mr. Gibson and Mrs. McAvoy studied the law and how they might be able to get some action on Merchant Mariners benefits. Additional aid came in the form of letters from ex-seamen to the Review Board and to Congress from three alumni of the USMMA. Newsletters were sent from merchant marine veterans organizations. Significant help came about this time from Capt. Lane Kirkland, President of the AFL/CIO in position and financial support. Lane Kirkland was a WW II USMMA Cadet and then a ship's officer in the worst years of 1942 and 1943 when thousands were sunk.

1987 – In July, Joan McAvoy, on behalf of her firm's client, the president of District One of the Marine Engineers Benevolent Association, presented our case before the Federal District Court of Columbia. She charged that the Civilian/Military Review Board had an arbitrary and capacious manner in disapproving the "ocean going group" and the "invasion group." She stated there were inconsistent standards throughout the SAF Review Board in dealing with PL95-202. In October, Federal District Court Judge Louis Oberdorfer ordered the Review Board to approve the "invasion group" and re-evaluate the "ocean group" of Merchant Marine WW II. The new legislation dragged away the AFR Board kicking and screaming to the end. (Nonnie Kolkebeck, Kings Pointer/Spring 1998.

1988 – We received our DD 214 brown paper Coast Guard discharges in a paper bag with a tiny green folder listing our few benefits which were for medical treatment if we were "homeless or on welfare." I almost threw the bag and its contents in the trash in disgust. A good number of the Marines did so or made no effort to get their "worthless" discharge.

When FDR signed the GI Bill in 1944, he said: "I trust Congress will soon provide similar opportunities to members of the Merchant Marine who risked their lives again and again during the war for the welfare of their country." Stanley Willner and Dennis Roland and many other POWs were being starved and worked to near death in Changi Gaol by the Japanese. Following the war, Willner and Roland discovered how Merchant Mariners were treated in our country. Stanley Willner stated that the beginning of this quest is seen in Dennis's emotions prior to the *March of Forgiveness* which helped elicit Congressman Biaggi's support, but the first 20 years of his campaign were met with one frustration after another. Merchant Marine and the US Maritime Service were official US Government services by law. Both were trained armed services by law, but that was ignored by Congress.

Senator Alan Cranston, chairman of the Senate Veterans Affairs Committee, opposed the amendments on the grounds that the Merchant Mariners and other civilians were "subjected to hazards and dangers while rendering valuable services in support of the nation's defense." Cranston cautioned against creating a precedent entitling persons classified as civilians to receive veterans' benefits. During the next ten years more than 50 groups applied for veterans status. Fourteen were successful. In addition to Congressman Mario Biaggi, Dennis Roland was unrelenting in his pursuit of veterans' status for the Merchant Marine. Roland wrote to Rear Admiral Penrose L. Albright of the US Naval Reserve JAGC office seeking legal assistance in his fight. Albright responded in 1976 indicating that Roland was entitled to legal assistance as a retired Naval Officer. He died in December 1984, at the age of 76. Attorney Joan McAvoy filed a lawsuit on behalf of three plaintiffs: Stanley Willner, Ed Schumacher and Lester Reid. Judge Oberdorfer ordered that the plaintiffs' motion be granted. In my call to Stanley Willner a couple of years ago, he stated that he is the only survivor of those involved in that lawsuit. All of the others are now deceased. Mrs. Connie Heffern, who is working on this book with me, spoke with Stanley Willner by phone a few weeks back. He said he remembered her and me after a few words with him.

The AMMV (American Merchant Marine Veterans) was formed in 1982 and still has 65 chapters scattered throughout the country. The first chapter was named Dennis Roland in respect for his long efforts to gain veterans status for the WW II Merchant Mariners. Membership has increased dramatically due to younger descendants of the veteran Mariners as well as those who joined in honor and respect for the Mariners losses and their major part in keeping our country free. The AMMV formed a "Just Compensation Committee" and was successful in getting two bills introduced into the US Congress. The first bill (HR 3729, introduced in 2004 by Representative Bob Filner of California) had the support of 140+ Congressmen.

Mr. Filner reintroduced the bill in 2007 as HR 23. It would, if enacted, pay each qualifying merchant seaman $1,000 a month with additional benefits for surviving spouses.

Opening Statement of the Honorable Bob Filner, Chairman, and a Representative in Congress from the State of California

April 18, 2007

Good Morning:

Honored Guests, Committee Members, and the brave men and women of the Merchant Marine.

This morning, our Committee continues its quest to correct a grave injustice heaped upon the gallant men of the Merchant Marine of

World War II. We are here today to shed some light on the mysteries surrounding the treatment that the Mariners suffered by being denied GI Bill benefits at the end of WW II and to find a way to compensate them, 60 years later, for their heroic deeds.

It is indisputable that the Allied Forces would not have been able to begin, sustain, or win WW II without the valiant service of the Merchant Marine. The ships they commanded carried troops, tanks, food, airplanes, fuel, locomotives and other critical supplies to every theater of war. Merchant Mariners participated from the beginning of the war both here and abroad–from the Atlantic coastal waters of the U.S. and England and from Normandy to Okinawa. In the concluding months of the war, as a part of Operation Magic Carpet, the Merchant Marine ships brought home over 3.5 million men deployed overseas.

During WW II, Merchant Mariners worked the most dangerous details and suffered the highest casualty rate of any of the other branches of service, <u>with nearly 1 in 26 dying in the line of duty</u>. A death rate of this magnitude is unimaginable and would not be tolerated in our current wartime endeavors in Iraq and Afghanistan. But the hulking, slow Liberty ships of the day were little more than sitting ducks for German U-boats and wolf packs. The government suppressed these dreadful numbers to ensure a steady stream of Merchant Marine volunteers needed to man the thousands of Liberty ships built in anticipation of the war effort. At this time I would like to submit for the record a joint letter of support from four Maritime Organizations wherein it quotes General Dwight Eisenhower, leader of the Allied Forces of WW II, who succinctly summed up the contributions of the Merchant Mariners, "When final victory is ours there is no organization that will share its credit more deservedly than the Merchant Marine."

Many of the Merchant Marine detractors claimed these men were draft dodgers. Nothing could be further from the truth. During WW II, there was active recruitment for men to join the U.S. Maritime Service (USMS) which trained the Merchant Marine. There were 37 official government recruiting offices set up around the country, with many offices located next to the Navy and Coast Guard offices. Untold numbers of these men were steered from the uniformed branches to join the Merchant Marine because as they were told by the recruiting officers, *that's where your country needs you.* Also, the Merchant Marine was ahead of its time because it was the only branch of service that did not discriminate based on race and that accepted men as young as age 16. The short story is that the country needed these men, and these men wanted to serve. The majority were unaware of the fine distinctions between the Merchant Marine, Navy, Coast Guard or other armed branches in terms of veteran status after wartime.

I believe their confusion was genuine. Congress passed the *Merchant Marine Act of 1936* to rebuild our Nation's Merchant Marine that had died out after WW I. Also in 1936, the U.S. Maritime Commission was established to oversee the rebuilding of this fleet. Along with the U.S. Maritime Service (USMS), the training arm set up in 1938, it grew the number of Merchant Mariners from 55,000 pre-war to over 250,000 men and opened training facilities around the country, including Sheepshead Bay and a full Merchant Marine Academy by 1942.

Once at war, in 1942, the U.S. War Shipping Administration, as an emergency wartime agency, took control of the purchasing and operation of commercial shipping vessels. Hence, all Merchant Mariners were under the auspices and control of this federal government agency. The Navy, as author Brian Herbert notes in his book, *The Forgotten Heroes*, exerted "de facto authority" over the

Merchant Marine service when it gained control of the Coast Guard–which in 1942 had become responsible for the inspection of Merchant Marine vessels and for the examination, licensing and certification of Merchant Marine personnel.

Trying to figure out who controlled the Merchant Marine and who should have made certain that the Merchant Marine of WW II were included as veterans is as futile as a game of "Who's on First?" The question is who lost in this bureaucratic, inter-agency shuffle? The answer is the Merchant Mariners who served selflessly despite all of the discord. I believe today–as I always have–and as Judge Louis Oberdorfer decided in 1988 in the seminal case brought by Stanley Willner and other mariners, (*Schumacher, Willner, et al., v. Aldridge*, 665 F. Supp.41 (D.D.C. 1987)) that these men had every reasonable expectation that they would be treated as veterans for their service to our nation and would be able to partake in any and all benefits that came with that status.

I want to emphasize that we are not here to establish whether or not these men are veterans. That was determined finally in 1988. We are here today to try to give them their due in <u>compensation</u>. Without question, the Merchant Mariners deserve our undying gratitude, not just in words but in deeds. Yet at the war's end, they received nothing. During WW II, if a Mariner died while in combat, his family was eligible to receive $5,000 from the War Shipping Administration. That's it. If he lived or was injured, he or his family received nothing. No GI bill–no readjustment pay, no unemployment benefits, no educational assistance, no housing or farm loan assistance, no VA hospitals or benefits, no priorities for local, state and federal jobs, not even participation in V-Day celebrations and parades. Not until 1988, after a hard-fought and ugly legal battle, did these men receive veteran status after 40 years of struggle. For 125,000 Merchant Mariners, it was already too late. What a travesty of justice.

Why these men were not included in the 1944 GI Bill of Rights remains a mystery. Was it because their chief champion, President Franklin Delano Roosevelt, a seaman himself and creator of the Merchant Marine Academy and the U.S. Maritime Commission and Service, died in April 1945? Were the Merchant Mariners caught up in the cross hairs of the politics of the day, of yellow journalism, of bad publicity, or rumors of strikes and draft dodging, of the anti-union sentiments, of the anti-communism scare, of racism, of competition with the uniformed branches, or was it just that a hybrid militarized organization got the short end of the stick when veteran status was being decided–disenfranchised without a voice at the proverbial table? Or, was it the confluence of all of these events? Will we ever know the real truth?

There are a few naysayers that will claim that the Merchant Mariners simply had dangerous jobs–jobs that would compare to the contractors of today in Iraq, paid by a private firm, paid a much higher rate than the average soldier and willing to assume the risks because of their high level of compensation. This is simply not true of the Merchant Marine of WW II. They were not paid more, but comparably and in some instances less, as the chart displayed to my left and attached letter indicate, which I would like to submit for the record. Moreover, they were only paid when they were working. When their ship was torpedoed or sunk and they were in shark-infested waters in a life boat, they were not being paid. POW, not paid. Wounded, not paid. Stanley Willner of the 1988 legal case, not paid. I know that a few of the witnesses today will expand on the wage issue, the greatest myth surrounding the Merchant Marine.

This is why I re-introduced the *Belated Thank You to the Merchant Marine of World War II Act of 2007*, H.R. 23. As many of my colleagues know, this bipartisan, bicameral bill will provide $1,000 a month to Merchant Marine veterans and to their surviving spouses to give them the real thanks that is long overdue.

Would this compensation correct the wrongs of the past? Does it mean that Merchant Mariners did not lose out on the advantages afforded to the other great men and women who served in WW II–namely through the 1944 GI Bill? NO. Does it lessen the hurt and betrayal they felt when they were not recognized by their country upon return from combat theaters around the world defending America? NO. Does it mean that men like Stanley Willner, who spent three and a half years as a Japanese POW, dropping from 135 to 70 pounds, working endless hours with little subsistence in nightmarish conditions building a railroad over the River Kwai, only to receive two weeks of medical care and little else, will ever be made whole? NO. This country needs to stop telling these men and their families, NO. This hearing, I hope, is but the beginning of "yeses" for belated compensation for these deserving souls.

Deserving souls like Stanley Willner, Ian Allison, Henry Van Gemert, Dean Beaumont, Frank Dooley, Dick Wiggins, Eldon Swopes, Bill Jackson, Eugene Barner, Burt Young, Warren Leback, Dennis Roland, George Duffy, Hank Rosen, Dan Horodysky, Marvin Willenburg, Joe Katusa, Joe Chomsky, Gerald Starnes, Mack Gleeson, Fernando Vallas, Bruce Felknor and Mr. Nicolich–those still with us today and for those who have *crossed the bar*.

Lastly, it is well worth noting that in February 2000, our friends to the North, Canada, recognized the service of its Merchant Marine by giving those who served two or more years, lump sum payments mostly in the range of $20,000. I would like to submit an article for the record that explains how this award was made.

Members of the Committee, we recently learned of the passing of one of the last veterans of World War I. When we heard the news, each of us felt a collective pride in our hearts for his service to our nation. That is why the designation of being a veteran is so important. When people hear the word, they think of the selfless service of men and women who are willing to put their lives on the line for their countrymen. That is what the Merchant Marine did selflessly, and that is why they received the veteran designation in 1988. That is why they deserve to receive belated <u>compensation</u> for their delayed ascension to veteran status.

President Washington got it right when he said, "The willingness with which our young people are likely to serve in any war, no matter how justified, shall be directly proportional as to how they perceive the Veterans of earlier wars were treated and appreciated by their country." We are here today to begin to right this tremendous wrong and to give the Merchant Marine veterans their due—in deeds not words.

Statement of Brian Herbert
HR-23 Hearing, April 18, 2007

When I saw the injustices suffered by the Merchant Marine, I wrote a book about the situation that was published three years ago, <u>The Forgotten Heroes</u>.

This nation owes a debt of honor to the men of the U.S. Merchant Mariner who served the Allied cause so valiantly in WW II. As a government and as people we have let these heroes down by denying military benefits to them. It is a shameful six+ decade in American history and a national disgrace.

From 1941 to 1945, the War Shipping Administration sent civilian seamen into the war zone transporting troops, bombs, tanks, planes, aviation fuel, torpedoes and other dangerous war materials. The typical Allied soldier needed eight tons of military supplies a year to sustain his ability to fight, and 80% of that was provided by the U.S. Merchant Marine. These brave men became a lifeline of the Allied forces overseas. Delivering essential cargoes, the Merchant Marine suffered more deaths per capita in WW II than any of the American armed forces, 32% higher rate than the U.S. Marine Corps.

Packed with military cargoes, the slow-moving ships of the Merchant Mariners were easy targets for German and Japanese naval and air forces. Torpedoes fired at merchant ships carrying ammunition or petroleum often caused explosions so immense that no trace was left of the vessels or their crews were ever found. Merchant ship duty was so hazardous that some men quit at the first opportunity and joined the armed forces – where it was safer.

Seamen suffered terribly. Medical workers and the survivors of the torpedoed oil tanker SS John D. Gill reported that the flesh of the burned seamen "would come off in your hands." When the SS Benjamin Brewster was torpedoed, a survivor described the screams of the dying, some boiled alive, others fried on the hot steel decks. One of the engineers was a "charred and misshapen figure" on a stretcher. Among those who survived disaster at sea, many suffered amputations or other disfiguring injuries.

At the end of the war, the men and women of the U.S. armed forces were honored with victory parades and the G.I. Bill, which gave them educational benefits and low interest loans. But the members of the U.S. Merchant Marine received none of that. Instead they were shunned, called draft dodgers, slacker bums and ridiculed as drunks. Many former seamen became derelicts without homes after the war like stray unwanted animals. Some committed suicide.

The reason for this involves politics, and a veil of lies and distortions that was placed over the achievements that have lasted their lifetime. It has even alleged that they were overpaid, perhaps the largest untruth of them all. How could they have possibly been overpaid when so many died and survivors were denied military benefits for their entire lives? These men, in fact, were grossly underpaid. They operated ships with skeleton crews. They performed the work of at least half a million men, more than twice their actual numbers, and were sent into battle with the equivalent of pea shooters on their decks.

During the war the Japanese Imperial Navy ordered their commanders to sink enemy ships and cargoes, and to "carry out the complete destruction of the crews." As a result, the American merchant seamen were machine-gunned in their lifeboats, tortured by submarine crews and thrown into shark-infested waters. Some of the survivors of the SS Jean Nicolet with their hands tied were left on the deck of a Japanese sub and drowned when the captain crash dived the sub. There are countless stories of Merchant Marine heroism and patriotism – too many in my allotted time.

****

In February 2005, Ian Allison and another member of the committee went to Washington, DC to push for passage and obtain a companion bill in the US Senate. They tried to get several senators to become the sponsor of a Senate companion bill, and none would take the challenge. Finally, Senator Ben Nelson of Nebraska agreed to introduce and sponsor the Belated Thank You to the Merchant Marines of WW II Act of 2007, S. 663. Senator Nelson was from a dry land, Midwest, agricultural state and was not a member of the Senate Committee on Veterans' Affairs.

The Just Compensation Committee made a comprehensive analysis of the limited benefits that were granted to the Merchant Marine veterans in 1988 in comparison to what the armed forces' veterans were receiving. In each example, armed forces' veterans received much broader coverage than the merchant seamen. Medical benefits to merchant seamen were reduced by a co-payment requirement, and burial benefits were less. In addition, WW II Merchant Marine vets never received the following:

1. Disability payments ;
2. Medical coverage for their families;
3. Educational benefits, including tuition, books, supplies and living expenses;
4. Financial assistance in home-buying;
5. Unemployment assistance and
6. Assistance in finding jobs.

AMMV asked for a "fair cash value in place of the unpaid benefits of the GI Bill" – both for the 43 years of no coverage and the very limited coverage granted after 1988. Merchant seamen war veterans in Canada received a lump-sum payment of $5,000 to $20,000 depending on service time as was done by our Allies, the Dutch, English, Norwegians, Russians and Greeks while we Americans received nothing from the richest country on earth. US armed forces gave POW medals to military prisoners, but Merchant Marine POWs received nothing. The Russians, of all people, did place medals on the chests of some of the American Mariners who made the most hazardous "Murmansk Run" to keep them from starving and supplying them with fuel, guns, ammunition, aircraft and all the materials of war.

After the war was over, we cadets had to go back to the Academy to complete our education. As I recall, we were given cardboard medals and a tiny, brass, metal pin from President Harry Truman that couldn't have cost more than one copper cent. Years later my two oldest grandsons wanted to see Grandpa's war medals. I was embarrassed and let them take my cardboard medals and forgot it. Just a few years back I called a retired captain from my class at the Academy about something, and he mentioned that a lady at MARAD had a budget for WW II veterans' medals. I didn't believe it, but old Charlie was always truthful, and what did I have to lose. For years those medals were sold on the market and black market at $30 each. I called the lady and she politely stated that I was eligible for several medals. She had my record and would send my medals to me at no cost.

Back to Senator Ben Nelson, our sponsor. The young staffer he assigned to S. 663 was way over his head in handling a Senate bill. Nelson was not one to work closely with his staffers. Washington lobbyists working with the US Senate bill will tell you that you must have a bill sponsoring Senator that pushes it in every way possible all the time to get it on the floor.

Too many of us American citizens and voters are not aware that the average time it takes to get a bill through the US Congress and signed into law is about 10.4 years and that hundred upon hundreds of bills "drop dead" in committees. Many of those bills are needed bills, and any Senator can stop the Senate operation at any time. A senator who was not going to run again for another six-year term and was a well-known, former major league pitcher in his earlier years tried this move to see if it would work. It did for a couple of hours before his fellow senators to start up the upper house of the US Congress.

Senator Ben Nelson's staffer resented me as the AMMV JCC Co-chair and Government Affairs Officer trying to get him to work on S. 663, the Belated Thank You to The Mariners of WW II Act of 2009 introduced on April 29, 2009 in Washington. That was also his sentiment with Burt Young, the Chapter leader in Lincoln NE, who lived near Senator Nelson's offices in that city. We were trying to get something happening on our bill.

After our lady lobbyist spoke with Senator Nelson, he asked Senator Daniel K. Akaka (D-HI), Chairman of the Senate Committee on Veterans Affairs, to allow him and others to speak at a hearing that included S.961. He was advised that he could speak at the hearing but he

Senator Daniel K. Akaka, Chairman Committee of Veterans Affairs comes over to greet & thank author Gerry Starnes AMMV Govt. Affairs for his testimony and trip to Washington DC.

would allow only one other person to speak who was knowledgeable of that bill. Senator Nelson asked whom he should find for that chore and was told by our lady lobbyist that AMMV's Government Affairs Officer was the only one to send.

The Hearing on Pending Benefits Legislation was held May 7, 2008. Senator Nelson was presiding over the Senate and asked to give his testimony on our bill as the first one doing so. Congressman Bob Filner, the Sponsor of HR 23, heard of the hearing from us and came in and had a conversation with Senator Akaka relative to the bills they had to work on together. Our bill was the last to be heard. Senator Akaka had asked Mr. Charles Dana Gibson, a well-known author of books on the Merchant Marine and was a young WW II veteran deck hand on sea going tugs towing barges, to be my adversary relative to my testimony.

139.5 pages of Senators and witnesses prepared statements make up the "Hearing " report, which is not worth the time it takes to read it; but Mr. Gibson's and my statements were all made before Senators Akaka, Ranking Member Richard Burr (R-NC) and a very few others present. Mr. Gibson worked with Mrs. McAvoy, who obtained our recognition as veterans, to get the same for his Army Transport Service in 1987. He is considered a Merchant Marine authority by a good many and is sure of it himself. Congressman Bob Filner addressed his fellow Congressmen upon reintroduction of HR 23 with some admiring words on their service.

Mr. Gibson is a recognized authority on the numbers that are commonly used in writing about the Merchant Marine losses, such as casualties, ships sunk, cargoes delivered, lost wages, benefits, destinations etc. Such records were not recorded by the WS Adm. for the purpose of security and it worked. Captains never knew where they were going until they read their sealed orders at sea. We could never tell the bar maids where we were going.

During the conversation with the senators after the statements were completed, Senator Akaka politely asked Mr. Gibson and me if we needed a financial benefit to maintain our standard of living. We both replied in the negative. I did what is not done with a senator. I interrupted his speaking and asked if I could speak to him on a matter bothering me. Our lady lobbyist, the AMMV News lady editor and my wife almost fainted. My age and the Senator's were about the same, and I reasoned that an old gentleman could speak respectfully to another old gentleman if he needed to do so. The Senator politely said, "Go ahead." I said, "Senator, for every WW II veteran Merchant Mariner like Mr. Gibson and me who has fortunately been successful, there are at least 100 poor former Mariners out there who are having difficulty putting bread on the table and a gallon of gas in his old car." He nodded his head in acknowledgment.

In my final statement to Senator Akaka, I said, "Senator, all the numbers and statements made have nothing to do with the question of this bill. The question is, "Did we earn the recognition and benefits we seek in helping to keep our country free?" He came to me after the hearing and shook my hand and thanked me for my trip to Washington *and did nothing toward putting our bill on the Floor*. There was no Mark Up of our Merchant Marine bill in the Senate Committee on Veteran's Affairs.

Senator Nelson and his Staffer had no alternative but to join the group of others in trying to get their bill attached as an Amendment to a bill that had to be passed into law to keep the government going. Of course, it was rejected in the time limit of such actions.

When Congressman Bob Filner reintroduced HR 23, Speaker Nancy Palosi suggested he remove the living spousal provision to reduce the cost of the entitlement and make it more acceptable.

In the very early spring of 2009, Senator Inouye, Chairman of the Appropriations Committee, and Senator Akaka arranged to obtain $198 million from the $786 billion Stimulus Package that was supposed to be used only to create jobs. This funding was an upgrading of the WW II Filipino veterans benefits that were promised them. They worked backwards by introducing and passing the bill in the Senate and then quietly introducing it in the House where it passed with some 9,900+ "earmarks." Senator John McCain and Congressman Steve Buyer were the only Congressional critics, and President Obama signed it into law on February 17, 2009. A very few American tax payers knew that the Philippines became a sovereign nation in 1948. Akaka placed a "hold" on our Mariners bill. We old Mariners remembered the Filipinos fought alongside of American soldiers and did not oppose their financial benefit. However, the Filipinos were fighting in the back yards of their own country while we fought all over the world to supply our and our allies fighting men with all their needs at the fronts.

As Merchant Mariners we had some wasted thoughts that perhaps we would also be given our benefits as suggested by FDR in 1944. We asked if that was a possibility and were informed that, "every penny in that Stimulus Package was already assigned to some individual or group."

The Hawaiian Islands trio of Senators Inouye, Akaka and Secretary Eric.K Shinsecki were the Champions of the Filipinos WW II benefits. The Filipinos were granted $198,000 and the Americans received $ 0.00. There was a distribution office quickly set up in Manila and other sites. Non-US citizens were given $9,000 and US citizens received $15,000. Filipinos have been getting a list of things for years and years such as burial rights, health care, disability benefits and many other things that American vets do not get from the Veterans Affairs Committees. I believe the Secretary and commit-tee assumed at this late date that approximately 21,000 would file a claim. The number was about 41,000 seeking a bonus, and they ran out of funding.

April 29, 2009: Chairman Akaka at 9:30 a.m. called his invited guests to order: Those speaking relative to our S. 663 Merchant Mariners bill were Director, Compensation Pension Service, Veterans Benefits Administration;

Assistant Director, National Legislative Services; Ranking Member Senator Richard Burr (R-NC) and others including the ever present and never a supporter, the VFW. The (AP) recently reported that four men were arrested in a VFW shooting outside the Veterans of Foreign Wars post in central FL that killed three.

The Director of Compensation & Pension Service stated: "Merchant Mariners and their survivors are already eligible for benefits based on such service." "This is not true," I thought as a ship's officer and gentleman. My fire and water tender would shout loudly, "It's a damn lie." As usual, the cost was deemed excessive and our being legal vets were questioned. Senator Burr sits up there beside Chairman Akaka and participates a little, writes fed letters to his constituents and does nothing to support the Mariners. As a congressman he did nominate my cousin's son for an appointment to the USMMA who has done very well as transportation officer for the Army in Afghanistan.

No one in the AMMV and anyone who support them was invited to this Hearing; but they erred a bit in inviting the Assistant Director, Veterans Affairs and Rehabilitation, The American Legion. "The American Legion has no standing on this piece of legislation. However, it is the general policy of the American Legion to voice concerns about provisions which set up one class of veterans in an exclusionary manner to other groups or classes of veterans. It has long been The American Legion's position that a veteran is a veteran regardless of branches of a service or occupational specialty. All of the men and women who have answered the call to serve their country are equal veterans and thus deserve equitable treatment under the law."

Senator Ben Nelson reintroduced our bill as S. 663 on April 29, 2009. My letter of July 9, 2010 from Chairman Akaka states that it was not considered for being sent to the full Senate for action, but he is not blocking the bill or opposing any member taking such actions. His concern over the legislation related to the precedent it would set relative to the many other groups who were not members of the US Armed Services during WW II, and he was also concerned about creating a benefit not based on disability.

Senator Nelson assigned a very capable lady, his Counsel for Military Affairs, who came from the Air Force. Ann worked well and hard with me for months, but we got nowhere.

Senate Majority Leader Senator Harry Reid assigned Col. Robert Herbert, an Air Force pilot on his staff, to be my contact relative to his support of our Bill S.663. I had an earlier letter from the Senator which stated that he would support the bill. Our two volunteer lobbyists had met with Col. Herbert and were quite impressed with his knowledge of legislation in Washington.

His e-mail of June 1, 2009:

> "Senator Reid is still committed to passing the Merchant Marine legislation, and he will bring it up at an appropriate time when we have the votes to move it from the Committee and pass it.
> What Senator Reid will never compromise in his fighting for Nevada's veterans, and your e-mail made references that were clearly out of line. I encourage you to consult your lobbyists about the legislative process and help us get the votes out of Committee instead of beating up a champion of your bill."

Of course, I had consulted my lobbyists and I admired Col. Herbert as an officer and a gentleman. I believe he sought a Cabinet position but didn't make it. In the 2010 election, Senator Reid appeared to be going to lose to a lady candidate. He was said to have gotten about $90 million in campaign funds and won reelection quite comfortably, and there was never a word on the Merchant Marine bill or much of anything else.

Senator Inouye had long been considered a friend of the Merchant Mariners and the Academy. His letter of February 7, 2008 ends with, "As Chairman of the Senate Appropriations Subcommittee on Defense and a member of the Subcommittee responsible for Veterans Affairs, you can be assured of my support of this Act." At the November 19, 2009 meeting with the Chairman by the NAUS (National Association for Uniformed Services) President and Legislative Director held in the Capitol office of the Senate Appropriations Committee, Senator Inouye acknowledged his promise but said he had to defer to Senator Akaka's wishes. It appears the Filipinos' $196 million appropriations preceded the authorization on this legislation.

Senator Akaka declined any meeting and suggested that the NAUS Officers meet with his Veterans Affairs Committee Majority Staff Director and his Hawaiian entourage who were belligerent and disrespectful of the NAUS gentlemen who represented American Merchant Mariners. They regarded the Merchant Mariners as worthless drunks and bums that sailed on ships and resented any comparison to Filipinos in US service. He parades himself as a former Naval officer of ten years.

Akaka liked to say our bill was not funded. Bob Filner had set up a Merchant Mariner Equity Compensation Fund in 2009-2010. We are often insulted by members of our Senate and House and their staff leaders when addressed in the manner of our being uneducated constituents they have to tolerate. We all know that the U.S. Senate can provide funding for any bill for any cause they care to support.

Our S.663 died in Akaka's Committee. No one in the Senate committee would support it. In the 2011 Republican takeover of the House, our Florida boy, Jeff Miller, became the Armed Services Chair in the Veterans Affairs Committee. Congressman Miller had cosponsored our bill HR 23 two or three times, and we thought Jeff might find a way to help us. He apparently knew nothing could be done and HR 23 went into the Subcommittee on Disability Assistance & Memorial Affairs with seven or eight members, none of which were from FL. I spoke at length from the heart with the Majority Staff Director who was all for us, but there was just no money to be had and nothing transpired. He asked that I wait about three months to call him and perhaps something positive might happen. I did not expect anything, but called as a courtesy and could not get my party on the phone. Finally, two young girls answered on his phone; they knew absolutely nothing, but they thought the gentleman was a Marine Reservist and had been called up for duty and was going to Afghanistan.

In the first week in January 2011, Congressman Bob Filner, Ranking Member of the Veterans Affairs Committee, reintroduced HR 23. He had found out that Senator Akaka had been asked to give up the chairmanship in favor of Senator Patty Murray (D-WA) who had supported us in the past. Her father was injured in and was a veteran of WW II.

Senator Ben Nelson (D-NE) waited a while but then said in public he would sponsor us Merchant Mariners again, but then he said no when he realized he just might not be reelected and decided not to run. Senator Nelson had personally persuaded the two Maine Republican Lady Senators to vote the two needed votes in the Senate to pass the disliked Obama Care bill.

Senator Murray was appointed the chairlady of the six Democratic members of the Super Committee, and called the "dirty dozen" and worse names along with the six Republicans. They were unable to agree on discretionary spending and avoid "sequestration." Rather than ending the threat of sequestration, they failed and the Super Committee triggered it.

As of the 2012 presidential election, nothing has come from the Senate or House Veterans Affairs for months, and no response has been received from constituents' inquiries. We are "dead in the water" as of this writing.

On Thursday, November 15, 2012, Senator Patty Murray announced she will step down as chair of the Senate VA Committee to seek the chairmanship of the Senate Budget Committee in the 113th Congress, filling a vacancy created by the retirement of Chairman Senator Kent Conrad (D-ND). Her move will provide an opportunity for Senator Bernard Sanders (I-VT), who caucuses with the Democrats, to become chairman of the Veterans Committee.

Murray says she would remain a member of the Veterans Committee and stay active on it. "They have not gotten rid of me," she joked.

Congressman Bob Filner ran for Mayor of San Diego, won narrowly, but has since resigned.

We now have some information that Sixtus Petraeus, the father of General David Petraeus, who was born in the Netherlands and came to the U.S. in the 1930s. He joined and served in the U.S. Merchant Marine during WW II on a Liberty ship. As the Captain, he singlehandedly extinguished a fire on the vessel that could have destroyed it. He was awarded the Meritorious Medal, the second highest honor given out by the Merchant Marine. It was one of the few handed out to any Mariner by the War Shipping Administration.

Since 2000, Akaka has sponsored legislation to afford sovereignty to the native Hawaiians. In April 2006, he was selected by <u>Time</u> magazine as one of "America's Five Worst Senators." The article criticized him for mainly authoring minor legislation, calling him "master of the minor resolution and the bill that dies in a committee." *This factual statement could not be better told.* Senator Daniel K. Akaka has never mentioned the fact that the Merchant Mariners Liberty Ships hauling food stuffs to the Hawaiian Islands all during WW II kept him and the other citizens from the fear of starving to death. Senator Akaka is retiring at the end of this current term.

From the <u>Wall Street Journal</u>, we are reminded that the late Senator Daniel K. Inouye, a hero of WW II who lost his right arm in an assault on a German machine gun nest as a platoon leader, has passed away at age 88. He served as a Democrat in the US Senate almost 50 years, keeping a low profile. As the son of poor Japanese immigrants, he thought of himself as more American than Japanese. He relished his role as the island's "King of Pork." He was one of the most ardent defenders of "earmarks" where the State of Hawaii's economy depends on federal dollars for a fourth of its income. He and his close friend, the late Senator Ted Stevens (R-AK), vied to see who could get the most earmarks into spending bills. Hawaii's first congressman put the Island on the political map and held them there for half a century, according to the WSJ.

With Congress under pressure to reduce discretionary spending in recent years, Mr. Inouye, as committee chairman, reluctantly declared a moratorium on earmarks in 2011.

As previously stated, I had contact with the good Senator for a few years. He promised me in a letter that he would stay with me in support of the Merchant Marine bill in the Senate. He was always interested in veteran affairs and was admired by everyone who was saddened by his passing. Senator Inouye never denied his promise, and he said he was committed to Senator Akaka's wishes. Unfortunately, those wishes were the obvious intent and actions to provide every available penny to the Filipino WW II veterans and their families whose US benefits needed an increase.

Merchant Marines Unfairly Excluded from the VFW
Franklin Press, Franklin, NC
6/2/10

> During World War II, there was a saying that it took ten men behind every man at the front. So, based on that statement, I am sure that a lot of servicemen in WW II, even if they were overseas,

didn't mean that they were in harm's way. But a Merchant Seaman during the war was immediately in harm's way as soon as he left port.

The Merchant Marine had the highest loss of men of any service in WW II. One in every 26 men was lost. If his ship was sunk, pay stopped; if a prisoner of war, pay stopped; if ashore waiting for another ship, no pay. All men were volunteers; many were 4Fs, under age, or over age for the draft, and also not allowed into the USO clubs. They were allowed to join the American Legion, but not the VFW.

I contacted the National VFW in Kansas City and there was a very poor excuse as to why a Merchant Seaman is not allowed to join the VFW: He was not military service. I would surely like to know whom they thought supplied them with the war material to fight the war.

Joe Foreman, WW II Merchant Seaman Veteran
Franklin

National Association for Uniformed Services

5535 Hempstead Way
Springfield, VA 22151-4094

May 25, 2010

The Honorable Barack Obama
President of the United States
The White House
Washington, D.C. 20500

Dear Sir:

On behalf of the National Association for Uniformed Services (NAUS), I write to strongly urge you to recognize finally, completely, and honorably, the service given in harm's way during World War II by members of the U.S. Merchant Mariners. I urge you to assist us in Senate passage of S.663, the Belated Thank you to Merchant Mariners of World War II Act of 2009.

The House has already approved its version of the bill, under the leadership of Speaker Nancy Pelosi and House Veterans' Affairs Committee Chairman Bob Filner, and as you recall when you were a Senator you cosponsored similar legislation.

When the GI Bill was signed in 1944, President Roosevelt said, "I trust Congress will soon provide similar opportunities to members of the Merchant Marine who risked their lives time and again during the War for the welfare of their country." Unfortunately, it took 44 years for veterans status to be conferred, long after other war veterans had used the generous benefits our nation provided and had received the medical care necessary to treat their wounds.

For all those years, the U.S. Merchant Marine Combat Veterans received no help from the Government they served and little to no recognition for wartime service to our country. They missed out on the GI Bill for their education, not to mention the cost of the medical care they underwent for the wounds, injuries and illnesses they experienced.

Nearly 300,000 men answered the call to train and serve in the U. S. Merchant Marine during WW II. Many never returned home and many others who did return came back with both physical and mental wounds. These men put their lives on the line for their country with 9,521 killed (or died from wounds), 12,000 wounded, 663 taken as Prisoners of War, and 66 who died in POW camps.

Fewer than 10,000 of these brave men, who challenged our enemy at sea and willingly risked life to help win the war, survive today. We ask you to support those now almost-ancient mariners whose heroic contribution as members of the ocean-going Merchant Mariners struggled to help secure the American victory in World War II.

The National Association for Uniformed Services asks you to encourage the Senate to take the right course. On behalf of a grateful nation, we urge you to request that the Senate honor these brave men with final passage of The Belated Thank You to the Merchant Mariner Combat Veterans of World War II.

Time is running short for a final thanks to the Merchant Mariner of World War II. We hope not to squander this opportunity. Thank you for your leadership and continued support for America's veterans.

Sincerely,
WILLIAM M. MATZ, JR.
Major General, US Army, Retired
President

Response to Questions Received

Dear Ms. Lura:

Please let me assure you that Mr. Ian T. Allison and I as the AMMV Co-chairmen of the JCC Committee and every member of that committee have done everything possible to push our bill through the US Congress during the past five years and more to no avail in the Senate. We were able to get our bill passed twice in the House. We testified before the House & Senate VA Committees and did well at both in Washington and joined the huge NAUS (National Assoc. for Uniformed Services) to obtain their help and expertise.

Our former National President Emeritus, Mr. A. J. Wichita and Current President, Mr. Morris Harvey, have diligently pursued every effort possible to get this six-decade + overdue bill to the floor of the US Senate to date. Few Americans are aware that in our system any single US Senator can stop the function of the whole government. One did so some time back for a couple of hours, just to show he could do it.

Senator Daniel K. Akaka, (D-HI), Chairman of the Senate VA Committee, let our bill die in committee on two different occasions. In early 2009, Senator Akaka with Senator Daniel K. Inouye (D-HI) arranged to take $198+ million for the benefit of the Filipino WW II vets from the $787 billion Stimulus Package that was supposed to create American jobs. That bill went backwards, starting in the Senate and then passing in the House along with more than 9,000 + *Earmarks*. The Philippines has been a sovereign entity since 1948. Senator Inouye promised me in writing that he would stay with me in support of our bill until it passed. I sent a copy to the President and Legislative Director of NAUS who asked him in person about the letter.

The bill HR 23 was again introduced in the House 1/5/ 2011. When Senator Patty Murray (D-WA) was made Chairlady of the VA Committee we thought we might have another chance. She had signed as a cosponsor and supporter before. Not even her constituents who know her personally have been able to contact the lady since her Democratic Chairlady position for the Super Committee, better known as the *Gang of 12,* that got nothing done. Senator Ben Nelson (D-NE) announced he would sponsor the Senate bill again then decided not to run for office again.

All we hear now from the bill in the Subcommittee on Disability Assistance & Memorial Affairs is they have no money for the bill. I'm trying to get VAC Chair, Jeff Miller (R-FL) to agree to a Lump Sum benefit of $20,000 to each eligible WW II Mariner and end this thing with some honor and dignity. They say for me to contact the Committee in May to see what the situation is then. It appears that our ranks are now only 6,000.

Our most serious problem has been getting our rank and file vets to contact their District Congress person again & again & again until they sign as a cosponsor of our bill. Our Mr. Perry Adams has spent hundreds of hours & dollars on this matter.

Congressmen and women only pay attention to their own district constituents who may or not vote for them every two years. In defense of our fellow Mariners, they did not get a GI Bill and a college education as the other services did such as our Navy armed gun crews on our ships. Therefore they are not comfortable writing letters, sending faxes or speaking with staff members in the Congressional Offices locally in their state or in Washington; and, of course, these are the elderly folks that have earned the benefit and most need the money to put bread on the table and gas in their old car.

Both Ian and I were senior engineering officers on the ships and were quite successful after the war and could afford to spend some of our own funds in this effort to support our crew men. We deal with the members of Congress which is a demanding undertaking. We also speak a lot with staffers. You can almost never get a member of Congress on the phone or to answer an email, fax or letter. At times we get to talk and shake hands with members of Congress.

If my request for the lump sum settlement makes it through, as is very unlikely, your stepfather might be eligible for the benefit. Does he have his USCG DD-214 discharge? They were mailed out in 1986. The subcommittee staffers say they like me because I know everything about ships and the bill, but they don't like my telling them what has to be done.

I hope this letter helps answer the questions you have in mind. I'm an alumnus of the USMMA @ Kings Point, NY. It is the only Federal Academy of the five that sends its cadets into combat zones. Just before the war ended I was glad to get into a combat zone and at $85/mo. get double pay for a short while.

Sincerely,
H. Gerald Starnes
BS, MBA, USCG Lic. Ch. Engr., AMMV JCC Co-chairman & Gvt Affairs